'*Philosophical Theology: The Basics* offers a clear and engaging introduction to philosophical theology. The authors guide the readers through the central questions, methods, and debates which have shaped Judeo-Christian thought, adopting an analytic approach, but gesturing towards wider horizons of thinking across different traditions and perspectives. The result is a text that will inspire as well as inform, inviting students to imagine how the field might expand, whilst giving them the tools to participate in this exciting journey. Essential reading for undergraduates and anyone seeking to grapple with the Big Questions.'

– **Fiona Ellis,** Professor of Philosophy, University of Nottingham

# PHILOSOPHICAL THEOLOGY

# THE BASICS

What is philosophical theology? How does philosophy relate to theology? Should theology be philosophical? This book explores answers to these questions from the ancient world to the present day, introducing the reader to the basic theories and thinkers in philosophical theology, within the Judaeo-Christian tradition.

The book guides readers through the basic theories and thinkers in Western philosophical theology from Plato to Plantinga, presenting key concerns that have led to debates within secular and Christian philosophy throughout history and encouraging readers to engage with these debates. It explores theories and schools of thought that have been developed to try and answer some of the most pressing questions in philosophy and theology across the following areas:

- faith and knowledge
- arguments for the existence of God
- mysticism
- religious language and experience
- the soul and life after death
- good and evil
- conscience and religious ethics
- human freewill
- divine providence and miracles

Accessibly written, this book is an ideal starting point for anyone seeking a full introduction to philosophical theology as well as broader themes in philosophy of religion and systematic theology.

**Dr Dafydd Mills Daniel** is Lecturer in Divinity, University of St Andrews. Previously McDonald Lecturer, University of Oxford, he is the author of *Conscience and the Age of Reason* and, with David Mills Daniel, *Briefly: 25 Great Philosophers from Plato to Sartre, Briefly: Nietzsche's Beyond Good and Evil* and *AS/A2 Ethics and Moral Philosophy*. His BBC radio documentaries include *Where Do Human Rights Come From?* and *Sir Isaac Newton and the Philosophers' Stone.*

**Dr David Mills Daniel** is the creator of the *Briefly* series of books on leading figures in the history of Western philosophy, from Plato and Aristotle to Bertrand Russell and A.J. Ayer. A former headmaster, researcher at the University of Leeds and A-level chief examiner, his books include *Briefly: Aquinas' Summa Theologica, Briefly: Descartes' Meditations on First Philosophy, Briefly: Hume's Dialogues Concerning Natural Religion, Briefly: Kant's Critique of Practical Reason, Briefly: Kierkegaard's Fear and Trembling.*

## The Basics

BIBLE AND FILM
*MATTHEW S. RINDGE*

RELIGION AND FILM
*JEANETTE REEDY SOLANO*

SECULARISM
*JACQUES BERLINERBLAU*

NEW RELIGIOUS MOVEMENTS
*JOSEPH LAYCOCK*

FILM MUSIC
*KENNETH LAMPL*

JEWISH ETHICS
*GEOFFREY D. CLAUSSEN*

QUAKERISM (SECOND EDITION)
*MARGERY POST ABBOTT AND CARL ABBOTT*

SIKHISM
*NIKKY-GUNINDER KAUR SINGH AND ELEANOR NESBITT*

ORTHODOX CHRISTIANITY
*NICHOLAS E. DENYSENKO*

FEMINIST THEOLOGIES
*SUSAN M. SHAW AND GRACE JI-SUN KIM*

QUEER THEOLOGIES (SECOND EDITION)
*CHRIS GREENOUGH*

PHILOSOPHICAL THEOLOGY
*DAFYDD MILLS DANIEL AND DAVID MILLS DANIEL*

For more information about this series, please visit: https://www.routledge.com/The-Basics/book-series/B

# PHILOSOPHICAL THEOLOGY

# THE BASICS

Dafydd Mills Daniel and David Mills Daniel

Routledge
Taylor & Francis Group
LONDON AND NEW YORK

Designed cover image: Getty Images

First published 2027
by Routledge
4 Park Square, Milton Park, Abingdon, Oxon OX14 4RN

and by Routledge
605 Third Avenue, New York, NY 10158

*Routledge is an imprint of the Taylor & Francis Group, an informa business*



*British Library Cataloguing-in-Publication Data*
A catalogue record for this book is available from the British Library

*Library of Congress Cataloging-in-Publication Data*
Names: Daniel, Dafydd Mills author | Daniel, David Mills author
Title: Philosophical theology : the basics / Dafydd Mills Daniel and David Mills Daniel.
Description: Abingdon, Oxon : Routledge, 2027. | Series: The basics | Includes bibliographical references and index.
Identifiers: LCCN 2026011668 (print) | LCCN 2026011669 (ebook) | ISBN 9781032939742 hardback | ISBN 9781032939759 paperback | ISBN 9781003568414 ebook
Subjects: LCSH: Philosophical theology | LCGFT: Introductory works
Classification: LCC BT40 .D36 2026 (print) | LCC BT40 (ebook)
LC record available at https://lccn.loc.gov/2026011668
LC ebook record available at https://lccn.loc.gov/2026011669

ISBN: 978-1-032-93974-2 (hbk)
ISBN: 978-1-032-93975-9 (pbk)
ISBN: 978-1-003-56841-4 (ebk)

DOI: 10.4324/9781003568414

Typeset in Bembo
by Apex CoVantage, LLC

*To Mum/Jenny, Ed and Meg*

# CONTENTS

# INTRODUCTION
# WHAT IS PHILOSOPHICAL THEOLOGY?

The 20th-century English philosopher, A.N. Whitehead, once remarked that the history of Western philosophy is a series of footnotes to Plato. The same might be said of the history of philosophical theology, especially as Plato, the founder of Western philosophy, is also the first person we know to have used the word theology.

Theology (*theologia*) literally means God-talk, and Plato first uses the term in his *Republic* when criticizing how Homer and other ancient Greek poets talk about the gods. For Plato, the stories of Greek mythology are bad theology, or an inadequate way of talking about the divine, precisely because they are not philosophical. Philosophical theology, or God-talk guided by philosophy, would prevent poets like Homer from talking about the gods as jealous, violent and malicious, because they would realize, philosophically speaking, that the divine must be talked about as perfect, and the source of good and not evil in the world.

If the history of Western philosophy and philosophical theology is footnotes to Plato, perhaps it is endnotes to Plato's student Aristotle. While Plato gives us the first recorded use of the word theology, Aristotle, in his *Metaphysics*, gives us the earliest definition of the study of theology itself.

For Aristotle, theology (*theologikê*) is metaphysics or 'first philosophy'. It is a 'theoretical philosophy', along with mathematics and natural sciences, but, unlike them, theology is 'first science', because it deals with the question of whether there is a divine being or substance that comes 'prior' to the objects of mathematical and scientific enquiry themselves. Theology is the science of the divine

DOI: 10.4324/9781003568414-1

or first things. It examines whether there is another eternal reality above nature (super-natural) and beyond the physical world (meta-physical), and theorizes about what a divine being is like when it is separable from, prior to, and the potential cause of both mathematical truth and the empirical world.

In Plato and Aristotle, theology is necessarily philosophical. In Chapters 1 and 2 of this book, we shall debate whether theology can or should be philosophical. Is faith in God something different from knowledge as pursued in the other theoretical philosophies described by Aristotle above, or do all human quests for knowledge and certainty resolve into some form of faith or trust? Is faith in the divine rational or justified, not least in the sense that it is possible to produce reasoned arguments to prove God's existence, or do all arguments for the existence of God fail as both philosophical and theological arguments?

Chapters 3 and 4 turn to assess God-talk in the more literal sense of what it means to talk about and to experience the divine. If the divine is so different from and so other to everything else that exists, such that, as Aristotle puts it, the science of theology considers 'being as being', how is it possible to describe or to speak about God when the divine is a unique mystery that lies beyond the limits of human language and experience itself? Is it possible to establish objective, philosophically and scientifically rigorous criteria that help us to discriminate between real and imagined experiences of the divine, or is genuine religious experience measurable by something more subjective, like morality and conscience? If so, does this risk make both God and the ethics of what God commands personal but arbitrary?

Chapters 5 and 6 put being in relation to beings, or God in relation to the world. When Plato first used the word theology, it was to criticize unphilosophical God-talk that made the divine responsible for evil but doesn't the existence of evil in the world undermine God-talk altogether? If it is claimed that the world is in moral disorder due to human immorality, isn't it also the case that human beings don't genuinely have freewill when a perfect God must foreknow everything that we do? What about physical, as well as moral, disorder in the world? Isn't this something the divine should be able to correct through miracles, and in response to prayer, especially if there is such a thing as divine providence or God's plan for the universe itself? Or, is the main human hope salvation from this disordered world into one after? If so, what is it about being human that gives us the hope that there is something about us, or some part of us, that exists after death? And, if I die in this world, how can I be the same person in any afterlife that I am in this life?

Following Plato and Aristotle, this book introduces philosophical theology as the critical assessment of God-talk and reasoned discourse on divine things in what is sometimes called the Anglo-American tradition of analytic philosophy of religion, which, especially in the English-speaking world, has dominated the historical development and current study of philosophical theology as an academic field.

As a result, the chapters in this book are geared towards thinkers, concepts and debates within both analytic Western philosophy and Judaeo-Christian theology, broadly conceived.

Consequently, there is not space, in this basics book, to include discussion of a range of thinkers in the Western but continental tradition of philosophy (including, for example, Nietzsche, Sartre, and Heidegger), just as there is not space to include discussion of the rich range of thinkers, themes and texts in the various traditions of Eastern philosophy.

Also, although, unlike in what is called analytic theology, the focus and starting point of this book are not the philosophical criticism or defence of particular Christian theological doctrines, it is the case that, where particular theological doctrines are referenced as part of, or to illustrate, philosophical theological debates these will tend to be either Christian doctrines or religious doctrines that may not be exclusively Christian, but which are taken from a broadly Christian setting.

In order to go beyond the basics of the field of philosophical theology as introduced in this book, the Conclusion contains further reading that will enable the reader to pursue the key topics covered in that chapter into wider Jewish, Islamic, Hindu, Buddhist and continental philosophical and theological contexts

# 1

# FAITH VERSUS KNOWLEDGE?

Perhaps one of the most famous bets ever placed in the history of Western thought is Pascal's wager.

Blaise Pascal was a French 17th-century philosopher and theologian, and in one part of his book *Pensées* (*Thoughts*), he asked is faith worth the gamble?

Pascal decides it is, because the odds are so greatly in its favour. Why wouldn't you bet on God's existence, and have faith in him, when all you're staking is this finite life against an infinite one? To put it bluntly, if you lose the bet, you're dead anyway, so it doesn't matter. But, if you win, your reward is infinitely greater than what you gambled in the first place, so why not have a flutter!?

Of course, Pascal's wager takes a lot of dedication. It's not just a one-off, placing some money down on a roulette table and seeing if your number comes up. Instead, if you gamble on faith, you must devote your whole life to God.

The question for us here is not whether you should take Pascal's wager, but why Pascal describes faith as a gamble in the first place?

One answer to this question is that faith is a gamble because it is not knowledge.

Knowledge is what philosophers have traditionally called justified true belief. I have knowledge not only when I believe in something that is true or factually correct. To have knowledge what I believe must, in fact, be actually true or correct, but I must also believe that it is true or correct for justifiable reasons.

Rather than the claim, 'God exists', let's use as an example the claim, 'Water boils at 100°C'.

DOI: 10.4324/9781003568414-2

The claim 'water boils at 100°C' is true or factually correct: water does indeed boil at 100°C. But, why do I believe that it is true? How do I *know* water boils at 100°C? When it comes to *knowing* something, the key question is not only whether what I believe turns out to be true but whether I have grounds or reasons to justify my belief in what is true.

So, I believe 'water boils at 100°C'. But *why*? Let's say I believe that water boils at 100°C as a result of the evidence of the whole history of human beings repeatedly heating water to boiling point at 100°C, and the evidence of the continued use of my own kettle. Now I have a belief or truth-claim, 'Water boils at 100 degrees,' and I have evidence that justifies my belief in the truth of this claim. I *know* water boils at 100°C, not just because, it turns out, water does, in fact, boil at 100°C, but because I have good and clear reasons and evidence that explain or justify why I believe 'water boils at 100°'.

Now, let's say I believe 'water boils at 100°C' because I had a dream in which a talking mouse told me that water boils at 100°C. Well, I am correct, water does boil at 100°C, but it's not obvious that I have *knowledge* of when water boils, because it's not obvious that I had any good reasons or evidence to justify my belief about when water boils. My belief turns out to be true, but I just got lucky. I didn't have any good reason to *know* it was true, I'd have believed that mouse if he'd said water boils at 90°C!

Similarly, take this example: You and two friends have a choice between doors A and B, and behind one of these doors is a prize. One friend says that you should choose door A because they can see it from their bedroom window, and they watched the prizegiver place something behind door A. Another friend says you should choose door A because their favourite fruit is an apple which begins with the letter A. Both of your friends turn out to be correct, the prize is behind door A, but wouldn't you say only the first friend had knowledge, justified true belief, that the prize was behind door A, even though both were correct in their belief that the prize was behind door A?

## FIDEISM

The language I've used above of luck and prizewinning takes us back to Pascal's wager. If faith in God is a gamble then it is not knowledge or justified true belief. The claim 'God exists' is like the claim 'this set of numbers will win the lottery'. I *hope* both claims turn out to be true, and I bet on them being true, but I don't *know* they are true. I don't have any proof or evidence that justifies my belief in the truth of these claims to the extent that I can say I *know* they are true rather than *hoped for* as true.

Thanks to his wager, Pascal is sometimes counted as a fideist: someone who thinks that faith is not knowledge, because it is belief founded on trust and hope rather than evidence and scientific reasoning.

Elsewhere in his *Thoughts*, Pascal seems to confirm his fideism by distinguishing between two orders: the order of the heart and the order of the understanding.

Knowledge is part of the order of the understanding. When we develop science, mathematics, and philosophy, we are using our mind to build systems of thought about things we know or are justified in believing to be true based on proofs supplied by reasoning, argument and evidence.

Faith is part of the order of the heart. We can't prove that God exists; we can't use reason to justify our belief that he exists. Instead, we just feel in our hearts that God exists. As Pascal puts it, 'It is the heart which experiences God, and not the reason. . . . This, then, is faith: God felt by the heart, not by the reason'.[1]

But if faith isn't knowledge, if it is a gamble, if it is felt in the heart rather than justified by rational proof, does that mean faith is uncertain?

The language of a leap of faith or faith as a wager definitely makes faith sound uncertain. But this is not really the point for Pascal or a fideist. Fideism maintains that faith is certain, but it is not certain knowledge but certain trust.

While Pascal describes faith as a wager, it is only a gamble from the perspective of the order of the understanding and not from the order of the heart. As Pascal points out, there are lots of things that human reason and the order of the understanding can't completely know and explain. Can mathematical theories or scientific experiments adequately define or explain what it feels like to love? I certainly have these experiences of loving and being loved, and so I know that I am experiencing something called 'love', even if I cannot encapsulate in scientific reason what that experience is. So, what if I base my faith in God's existence on the experience I have of loving something out there through the order of the heart? Now, faith is based on something I know for certain in my heart, even though it is not based on something I know for certain through rational arguments.

## AGNOSTICISM

The fideist claims to know God exists on the basis of a special feeling, for example what the 19th-century German theologian Friedrich Schleiermacher called 'the feeling of absolute dependence'.[2] And, it is in trusting this feeling, to the order of the heart, that I know God exists.

But suppose I want to trust my mind rather than my heart, and I want knowledge in the strict sense of the word. I want to say that my belief is reasonable because I can show objective evidence rather than only subjective feelings. I want faith to be part of the order of the understanding, not just the order of the heart.

Well, for Pascal, the problem with trying to make faith part of the order of the understanding is that you get stuck in an impasse or deadlock:

> This is what I see, and what troubles me. I look on all sides, and everywhere I see only darkness everywhere. Nature presents to me nothing which is not matter of doubt and concern. If I saw nothing there which revealed a Divinity, I would come to a negative conclusion; if I saw everywhere the signs of a Creator, I would remain peacefully in faith. But, seeing too much to deny and too little to be sure, I am in a state to be pitied.[3]

Pascal wants to know whether or not he should believe in God's existence. He uses reason to work out arguments for and against. But the problem is that there are equally strong arguments for and against so he is stuck. Should he believe or not believe? In order to break the deadlock, Pascal gives up on proof and the order of understanding and gambles, trusting to a different order, the order of the heart.

However, there is another option available to Pascal: he could just remain stuck in the impasse, and not bet on God's existence one way or the other. In other words, Pascal could just be agnostic.

The phrase agnosticism was first coined by the biologist Thomas Huxley. According to Huxley, agnosticism insists 'it is wrong for a man to say that he is certain of the objective truth of any proposition unless he can produce evidence which logically justifies that certainty'.[4]

So, in some ways, Pascal's wager does sound consistent with agnosticism. Pascal admits that there is no evidence within the order of the understanding that logically justifies belief in God. Pascal can find evidence that both proves and disproves the proposition 'God exists'.

Why, then, is Pascal's wager fideistic rather than an agnostic?

Well, Pascal does what the agnostic thinks is wrong. He places his bet on God's existence even though he lacks logical justification. An agnostic would say that where we lack logical justification, suspend judgement and don't believe.

## ATHEISM

When reading the last sentence above, you might think that that also sounds like atheism: 'don't believe'.

Theism is the belief that there is a God. Atheism is the belief that there is no God. So when an agnostic says 'there's not enough evidence to believe in God' and 'don't believe in God without evidence', they seem to be saying the same thing as an atheist, don't they?

Well, not really. There is a key difference between agnosticism and atheism. Namely, that the agnostic can reject both theism and atheism. As Huxley puts it:

> Agnosticism puts aside not only the greater part of popular theology, but also the greater part of popular anti-theology. On the whole, the 'bosh' of heterodoxy is more offensive to me than that of orthodoxy, because heterodoxy professes to be guided by reason and science, and orthodoxy does not.[5]

The atheist and agnostic both agree 'belief in God isn't justified because there isn't any evidence for God's existence'. But the agnostic says that just because you can't prove there is a God doesn't mean you've proved there isn't one. The atheist goes further and says the lack of evidence for God means we should believe 'God does not exist'. The atheist may also argue that they have evidence which proves that God does not exist. But the agnostic remains unconvinced. For the agnostic, there is no evidence to finally prove or disprove God's existence one way or the other, and so both theism and atheism are acts of faith, because they both believe opposing truth-claims without any conclusive evidence either way.

## EVIDENTIALISM

So far, I've mentioned a few *isms*. In order to further reflect on what they mean and the relationship between them, it is useful to introduce another *ism*: evidentialism.

From its name, you may have guessed that evidentialism is the view that we are only justified in believing if we have evidence. The evidentialist position is effectively summarized by 19th-century English philosopher, W.K. Clifford: 'it is wrong always, everywhere, and for anyone to believe anything upon insufficient evidence'.[6]

Now, the next question is: what counts as evidence?

Well, if you are one of Huxley's agnostics or an atheist like Richard Dawkins, the evidence that counts is empirical evidence. Evidence gathered through direct experience and observation. The type of evidence we most commonly associate with the scientific revolution brought about by people like Sir Isaac Newton. Newton famously declared, 'I frame no hypothesis'. What he meant by this was that he wouldn't assume the truth of any theory or hypothesis about the world without testing whether or not that theory or hypothesis works in the world.

In the context of philosophical theology, the hypothesis 'God exists' is a truth-claim about reality. It is the claim that the statement 'God exists' is an objective fact. If the statement 'God exists' is a factual claim about reality, it seems reasonable to expect that it is a hypothesis we can prove with evidence taken from reality. But what happens when that evidence is lacking?

Well, the fideist says, believe anyway, trust your heart, take the leap of faith. The atheist says, do the opposite, without evidence, deny faith, disbelieve. The agonistic says, without evidence, suspend belief and disbelief altogether.

But the agnostic can actually make an even stronger claim still. She can say that it is simply nonsense to debate whether God does or doesn't exist, precisely because it is a metaphysical, rather than a physical, question.

As God is a being who is above nature (super-natural) and beyond physics (meta-physical), then it seems he is something whose existence can be endlessly debated precisely because there is no final physical or natural evidence to prove whether or not he exists. We cannot prove whether God exists or what he is like in the same way Newton proved gravity through scientific experiments, so what's the point of talking about God at all?

Here again, we can see the differences and connections between certain types of agnosticism and atheism.

On the one hand, the atheist and agnostic disagree. The atheist thinks it is possible to prove the statement 'God does not exist', when the agnostic thinks that it is not possible to prove either the statement 'God does not exist' or the statement 'God does exist'. Both are metaphysical questions that will always lack absolute physical proof, so believe neither.

On the other hand, agnosticism can undermine theism or belief in God just as atheism opposes it. If the agnostic says it is *meaningless* to claim either 'God exists' or 'God does not exist', because both are *nonsense* metaphysical claims, then this is perhaps a more devastating blow to theism than atheism. At least the atheist seems to take the theist position seriously, and enters into (often heated!) arguments with them, attempting to counter their belief in God with rival evidence. By contrast, the agnostic can say, 'I don't even understand what you mean when you say "I believe God exists", it is an entirely meaningless statement.'

## LOGICAL POSITIVISM

The stronger type of agnosticism I've described above is a version of logical positivism particularly associated with the 20th-century English philosopher, A.J. Ayer.

Ayer thought that genuine 'philosophical inquiry' should lead to 'the elimination of metaphysics'.[7] Metaphysics is not what good philosophy should be engaged with, precisely because metaphysical claims can never be verified by experience or empirical data.

Ayer made this point by emphasising what he called 'the empirical verification principle', according to which statements are only meaningful if they're capable of being verified by experience.

So, to use one of Ayer's examples,[8] to debate whether or not there are mountains on the moon is meaningful because it is possible to verify empirically whether moon-mountains exist: they are physical things which we can physically see through telescopes. By contrast, to debate whether God exists is meaningless because it is not possible to verify empirically whether God exists: he is a metaphysical thing which we cannot see physically through telescopes.

As a result, *theologia* or God-talk (see Introduction) is meaningless and senseless in a way that moon-mountain talk is not. When I engage in 'God-talk', I am not engaged in a discourse which has meaning or significance; it is not what philosophers call truth-apt, because it is not something that is capable of being empirically verified as either true or false.

Notice that Ayer is not saying that such statements as 'God exists', 'miracles happen', 'I have a soul' are true or false. He's saying they are senseless and unintelligible, 'meaningless' and 'nonsense': 'For we shall maintain that no statement which refers to a "reality" transcending the limits of all possible sense-experience can possibly have any literal significance'.[9]

## NONCOGNITIVISM

Ayer's logical positivism seems to deal a devastating blow to theism. Presumably, anyone who is a theist, who claims 'I believe that God exists', is claiming both that God really does exist and that it is meaningful to say that he does.

However, the 'God-talker' can actually agree with Ayer in at least two ways, which I shall discuss as follows:

- Classical foundationalism
- Noncognitivism

Both of these approaches fundamentally disagree with each other but agree with Ayer's verification principle, even though they disagree with the conclusion he draws from it about religious belief and language.

## CLASSICAL FOUNDATIONALISM

One response to Ayer is to agree with his empirical verification principle, but say that, in fact, the statement 'God exists' satisfies Ayer's own principle and so is not meaningless.

Ayer insists that the statement 'God exists' is meaningless because it is not empirically verifiable. However, in Chapter 2, you will find a host of philosophical theologians who argue that 'God exists' is verifiable empirically, through such things as religious experience and observing design in the world.

Arguing for God's existence is usually a form of classical foundationalism, and classical foundationalism is itself a form of evidentialism, as previously discussed. Classical foundationalism maintains that all belief, if it is to count as knowledge, must be built on something which is certain as its solid foundation.

So, the foundation for the claim that God exists might lie in logic. We know by what is called *a priori* reason (that is, reason prior to or without the need for experience) that God exists in the same way we know 2 + 2 = 4. It is as absurd to say '2 + 2 = 5' as it is to say 'God does not exist', and the foundation for my belief that God exists is the same as the foundation for my belief that 2 + 2 = 4: it is self-evidently true to reason, and so my foundation for believing it is reason itself.

Alternatively, the foundation for the claim that God exists might lie in empirical experience. We know by what is called *a posteriori* reason (that is, reasoning post or after experience), that the universe is comprised of a complicated system of laws of nature; we also know from experience that complicated machines, like watches, require a mind to create them. So, it is reasonable to infer from our experience of order in the universe that there is a divine mind who designed and created such order, in line with our experience of machines, which require a human mind to create them.

We shall discuss such arguments for God in more detail in Chapter 2 but note now that philosophical theologians who think it is possible to argue for God's existence oppose both Ayer's logical positivism and Pascal's fideism.

Theistic classical foundationalism agrees with Ayer that truth-claims must be verifiable, but, contrary to logical positivism, insists that faith is knowledge, precisely because it consists of truth-claims that can, in principle, be verified.

And, as faith is knowledge, fideism is also rejected, because faith is not a matter of trust and the order of the heart but rational proof and the order of the understanding. For the theistic classical foundationalist Pascal doesn't need to wager, because there are arguments which prove God's existence and provide definite foundations to justify belief.

## NONCOGNITIVISM

Now, a completely different approach from classical foundationalism agrees with Ayer that faith is not knowledge but argues against Ayer that this is precisely what makes God-talk meaningful.

The 20th-century English philosopher, R. B. Braithwaite contends that a noncognitivist about religious language can follow Ayer, and agree that the claim 'God exists' is not truth-apt, but also maintain that the statement 'God exists' is significant rather than nonsense, because expressions of religious belief are meaningful even if they do not refer to a God that actually exists.

To appreciate Braithwaite's position, we need to recognise the difference between cognitivism and noncognitivism about religious language.

Cognitivism (from *cognito* = knowledge) is probably what most of us are thinking when we hear the statement 'God exists'. For a cognitivist, statements like 'God exists', 'God is good', 'God is powerful' are truth-claims. When someone says they believe these things, they are stating what they consider to be facts and announcing what they believe to be objectively true.

Fideism and classical foundationalism, as discussed above, are both cognitivist because they both believe that the claim 'God exists' is objectively true. A classical foundationalist thinks it is possible to use human reason to produce logical or empirical arguments to prove that God really exists out there in the world. A fideist also believes God really exists out there in the world, even if they deny that it's possible to produce arguments to prove God's existence. When Pascal says he knows in his heart that God exists, he is suggesting that his heart is giving him access to something that is objectively real, to a God that really exists. Similarly, when Schleiermacher refers to 'God-consciousness',[10] he is claiming there is some part of us which just knows God really exists, even if this certainty comes from feeling rather than rational argument.

By contrast, noncognitivism is the position that religious language is not factually significant. When someone claims 'God exists' they are not actually expressing an objective truth-claim or their commitment to a fact about reality. Instead, they are only expressing something that is true or meaningful about themselves.

For Braithwaite, expressing a belief about God is not expressing a belief which is meaningful because it is a claim about what is objectively real. It is expressing a belief which is meaningful because it reflects the subjective reality of an individual's own fundamental attitudes and view of life. Take the belief 'God is love'. In saying this, the believer is not committed to the belief that there actually is a God who exists and who is the embodiment of love. Instead, the statement 'God is love' is more like the statement 'Love is what I take to be the ultimate meaning and purpose of life itself' (for more on love or *agape*: see Chapter 4). Consequently, within noncognitivism, religious statements can be subjectively rather than objectively significant, because of what they say about an individual's own inner spiritual reality rather than because of what they say about outward physical reality.

## REFORMED EPISTEMOLOGY

One issue for Braithwaite's noncognitivism is that it makes God-talk meaningful, but only by making God-talk about the subjective truth of the believer rather than the objective truth of what the believer is talking about: God. Presumably, most believers, when they talk about God, are talking about something they consider to be real, in an objective cognitivist sense.

But if noncognitivism is problematic, and the claim 'God exists' really is a factual claim about reality, then we're still left with the question of whether there is evidence to justify belief in this objective claim? Shall we say faith has evidence and so is knowledge (theistic classical foundationalism), or admit that faith doesn't have evidence and so is trust and not knowledge (fideism)?

Well, there is another option: Reformed epistemology, as particularly associated with the American philosopher, Alvin Plantinga. What makes Reformed epistemology distinctive is that it rejects evidentialism, logical positivism, classical foundationalism and fideism all together, and says belief in God is rational, and counts as knowledge, even without evidence.

According to Plantinga's Reformed epistemology, we are rationally justified in claiming that we know that God exists, even if we don't have evidence to prove it, because there are lots of things we believe that we know certainly but without evidence.

A key word here is *sense*, in at least three senses (as it were!):

- Our *five senses* of sight, smell, touch, hearing, taste
- What the 18th-century Scottish philosopher, Thomas Reid referred to as *common sense*
- What the 16th-century Reformation theologian, John Calvin called *sensus divinitatis* or sense of divinity

Let's take *1. Our five senses*, and use the example of sight. Let's say you are out walking in some vast woodland and you come across an old cottage. Because you see that cottage, you know it is there. Wouldn't it now be odd for you to ask yourself for further evidence to justify your initial belief? You don't argue to yourself that the cottage exists, you don't infer the cottage exists because you see it. Instead, it is just in seeing it that you know it is there. Your belief in the building's existence is rational, but not because you've made an argument, with evidence, but because it is a belief that comes spon taneously and immediately with seeing it.

Let's take *2. Common sense*, where the common sense philosophy of Reid is often mentioned by Reformed epistemologists. Now, you come back from your walk and tell your best friend about the old cottage, and he says, 'How do you know it was an old cottage, how can you prove the past exists, how do you know aliens didn't make that cottage yesterday? In fact, how can you prove you didn't dream the whole thing?' Well, when you think about it is difficult to prove any of these things. But then you think a little more and realize it seems odd to even ask for proof of them, because you just know them as a matter of common sense without searching for evidence or proof. Common sense philosophy points out that we have various basic beliefs that we know to be true immediately, spontaneously and fundamentally, but without evidence. How do you know you're not dreaming right now? How do you know yesterday happened? How do you know your five senses reveal reality as it is and you're not being controlled by aliens? Well, you just do. You don't feel the need to prove the old cottage you see in front of you is real, because you just know it is there via your senses, you also don't feel the need to prove there is such a thing as space (near and far away), time (before and after) and causation (cause and effect), because you just know they are true by your common sense.

Let's turn to 3. Calvin's *sensus divinitatis*. The very name 'Reformed epistemology' signifies the influence of Calvin. The word epistemology means theories of knowledge (the subject of this chapter!), and the word Reformed means in the tradition of Calvinism. According to Calvin, all human beings have a natural sense that God is real. As Plantinga puts it,

> Calvin's claim is that God has created us in such a way that we have a strong tendency or inclination toward belief in him. . . . Calvin thinks, one who does not believe in God is in an epistemically substandard position – rather like a man who does not believe that his wife exists, or thinks she is likely a cleverly constructed robot and has no thoughts, feelings, or consciousness.[11]

What Plantinga is getting at here is that Calvin's *sensus divinitatis* makes it just as perverse to doubt the existence of God, as it would be to doubt your five senses or to doubt your common sense.

According to evidentialism, anyone who believes without evidence is in an epistemically substandard position, because they're believing something that they don't know. For the evidentialist, if you believe in God without evidence, you are epistemically substandard, because you are making a truth-claim, a claim to know something, without anything to justify or verify your belief. But, what if the evidentialist is just wrong? What if we don't need evidence for all our beliefs, because some beliefs are just basic? And, what if we don't require evidence of God before we believe in him, because belief in God is just basic via a sense, in the same way that belief in spatial dimensions and the material world is just basic via our common sense and five physical senses? Now, to doubt God's existence is epistemically substandard, because it is contrary to sense, in the same way as doubting whether the world is three dimensional, and believing that the tree I see over there is not far away by actually flat against my nose, is epistemically substandard, because it is contrary to sense.

Plantinga's point is that some beliefs are grounded and justified, even if they are not grounded in and justified by evidence. Sometimes, the ground that justifies our believing something is simply the immediacy with which we sense it. According to the evidentialist, belief in God is irrational and unjustified because it lacks evidence, but there are a number of things that we believe without evidence. Our belief that the tree we see actually exists and is over there is occasioned by seeing it through the sense of sight: it is just the sense of seeing the tree that is the immediate ground that justifies our belief that the tree is real and over there. Our belief that the God we perceive actually exists is occasioned by perceiving him through the sense of divinity: it is just the sense of perceiving God that is the immediate ground that justifies our belief that God is real and loves us.

## THE GREAT PUMPKIN OBJECTION

Now, you might have noticed, in the last sentence above, I dropped in two claims about God: that by *sensus divinitatis* we know both 'God exists' and 'God is love'. It is here that we encounter an objection to Reformed epistemology: what beliefs about God does it justify?

This objection is often called the great pumpkin objection, because what if I said I believe God is a great pumpkin? If belief in God is basic via *sensus divinitatis*, then isn't it the case that whatever this sense tells me I am justified in believing, such that no one can criticize anyone else's sense of God?

Well, let's return here to the analogy with the sense of sight. My sense of sight can go wrong, and may be lost or impaired. However, I don't just rely on my sense of sight alone but, for example, other senses that I have, and discussion with, and guidance from, other people.

For Plantinga, it is the same thing with my *sensus divinitatis*. It might ground my basic belief that there is a God, and even supply my sense of what this God is like, but it does not justify any superstitious belief I may happen to have. Calvin provides an example here. For him, paganism is not only proof that *sensus divinitatis* is universal in human beings but also proof that it is prone to error and in need of correction through both rational inquiry and divine revelation. Admitting that our common sense beliefs may require critical reflection in light of evidence is not the same thing as saying we need evidence to justify our basic beliefs. Through my sense of sight, I am justified in my belief that there is a tree over there, but I can reasonably debate how far it is over there and accept correction when my immediate sense that it is 5 feet away is shown to be misguided by my friend who supplies reasoned arguments to justify his view that it is 10 feet away. Similarly, to have what Plantinga calls warrant to believe, I must be aware, following Calvin, that my *sensus divinitatis* 'has been in part overlaid or suppressed by sin'.[12] So, like my potentially faulty sense of sight, my *sensus divinitatis* must always be open to correction and development. If I find I can't defend consistently my initial sense of God, that there is evidence to contradict it, and that another account of God is more convincing, I can and should admit that my immediate sense of God was wrong and work to adjust it.

## WEAK FIDEISM

In rejecting evidentialism, Reformed epistemology might sound a bit like fideism. Reformed epistemology agrees with fideism that we don't need arguments and evidence to justify belief in God. But there is a key difference between Reformed epistemology and fideism.

In fideism, faith is not based on reasoning; it is trust, not knowledge. But in Reformed epistemology, faith *is* knowledge, and it is rational. The difference between Reformed epistemology and evidentialism is that evidentialism says faith must have evidence to be rational, whereas the former says we don't have to infer or prove God's existence from evidence for it to be rational. Faith in God, like so many of our other beliefs, is rational on the basis of common sense, even without arguments to justify it.

Although Reformed epistemology resists fideism, it does help us to think about different ways of being fideistic.

Earlier, I described Pascal's wager as fideistic. Remember, Pascal thinks we lack the final piece of evidence to prove God's existence, so we can't say that we know for certain that God exists. As a result, faith is not knowledge or justified true belief – it is what Pascal calls a wager.

However, although all this sounds fideistic, we should note that it is what I'll call *weak fideism*, in at least two ways.

- When it comes to faith in God, the order of the heart takes over from, rather than opposes, the order of the understanding.
  In Pascal's wager, it's not that reason or the order of the understanding says 'don't believe' it's that our rational mind says 'I don't know, I can't decide because I see evidence both for and against God'. Faith and reason don't directly oppose each other; it is just that the certainty of faith belongs to a different order, the order of the heart, rather than the order of the understanding. So, Pascal might agree with Shakespeare's Hamlet: 'There are more things in Heaven and Earth, Horatio, than are dreamt of in your philosophy.' To take the leap of faith is not to contradict reason, but to move beyond the limits of reason: it is to trust to a certainty known within the order of the heart rather than within the order of the understanding.
- The order of the understanding is itself fideistic!

If strong fideism suggests that faith opposes reason, that faith and knowledge are two entirely different things, then Pascal seems only weakly fideistic because he suggests that knowledge is like faith, because, in the end, it resolves into trust:

> For the knowledge of first principles, as space, time, motion, number, is as sure as any of those which we get from reasoning. And reason must trust these intuitions of the heart, and must base them on every argument.[13]

What is Pascal getting at in this quotation? He is arguing that reasoning or argument in the order of the understanding depends on 'first principles', it does not establish through argument, evidence and proof, but assumes through trust, heart and faith.

One way to think of this is with reference to Immanuel Kant's 'categories of the understanding'.[14] According to Kant, we come into the world with the concepts of space and time just built into our minds. We don't try and prove space and time, we just seem to assume there is such a thing as space and time, and these structure our experiences of the world around us. Without the concept of time (one thing happens before, after, simultaneously with another) and space (one thing is close to, far away from, against another), we could not construct the entire edifice of theoretical mathematics, physics and engineering. But these complex theories, and the complicated technology and architecture they gave rise to, in the end rest on foundational categories and principles that we just assume rather than prove. It might be the case that I can prove the truth of a mathematical equation, but how can I prove there is something such as the number 6? I know that $3 + 3 = 6$, but where does the whole idea that there is such a thing as numbers come from? When I pile up stones, why do I recognize that pile as comprising a number of individual stones as well as being just one big pile? From where do I get the concepts of quantity and addition, space and time, more and less, near and far, old and new, and why am I so certain of them?

For Pascal, we are certain of them because they are 'first principles' of our hearts. Just things we trust in our heart about reality, in the same way we trust all this isn't a dream, and my best friend isn't a robot. Reason doesn't seek to prove the truth of these 'intuitions' of the heart, it takes them for granted and builds the edifice of the order of the understanding upon these fundamental truths we trust in our heart. So, although Pascal is fideistic in distinguishing between faith as part of the order of the heart and knowledge as part of the order of the understanding, he also maintains that, in the end, the order of the understanding depends on the order of the heart. So, at bottom, what we call reason and knowledge in fact rests upon faith and heart.

It's here that we might begin to wonder whether Pascal's fideism is not just weak, but so weak it is not really fideism at all, but something more like Reformed epistemology?

Pascal is like Plantinga, in the sense that he is criticising secular philosophers and scientists who 'impugn' faith in God as irrational and uncertain because it lacks evidence, when there are lots of fundamental beliefs or 'first principles' in secular philosophy, mathematics and science that also lack evidence and rest upon 'intuitions of the heart'.

However, there is a subtle difference of emphasis between these figures, which makes Pascal weakly fideistic and Plantinga non-fideistic.

Plantinga claims that faith is part of the order of the understanding, not the heart. The beliefs 'God exists' and 'I am not a robot' are not a matter of faith, but rational knowledge or justified true beliefs, because they are basic beliefs that it is reasonable to believe as a matter of common sense. Strictly speaking, for Pascal, neither of these claims counts as rational knowledge because neither can be objectively proven by reasoning, and so first principles in the order of the understanding ('space, time, motion, number') and in the order of the heart (God exists) both rely on faith and trust rather than reason and knowledge.

## STRONG FIDEISM

If Pascal's position is weak fideism, what about strong fideism? Well, a strong fideist would maintain that faith is irrational, that faith can, and even should, contradict reason and evidence, because there is no touchpoint or analogy between the order of the understanding and the order of the heart.

The 20th-century German theologian, Dietrich Bonhoeffer, illustrates a theme in strong fideism by distinguishing between the divine and human *logos*.

According to Bonhoeffer, the human *logos* is reason, which always seeks knowledge by means of the question 'how?'[15] How does this work, how did this happen, how can I understand this, how can I benefit from it? The divine *logos* is the Son of God, the second person of the Trinity, who becomes incarnate as Jesus Christ. It is in the incarnation of the divine *logos* that the human *logos* meets its limitation. In the incarnation, the divine *logos* confronts the human *logos* with the requirement that it surrenders its question 'how?' for the new question 'who?' Not *how* is it possible for Jesus to be both human and divine, *how* is it possible for a perfect and all-powerful God to become imperfect and weak human flesh, *how* is it possible for God to love everyone, even sinners, to the point of sacrifice? But *who* is God revealed to be in the incarnation and crucifixion and *who* am I called to be in imitation of this God who suffered on the cross for all human beings?

For Bonhoeffer, the change from 'how?' to 'who?', from the human *logos* to the divine *logos*, marks the change from '*sicut deus* man' to '*imago dei* man'.[16] '*Sicut deus* man' are human beings who seek to know how they can be *like God*, how they can acquire enough knowledge to gain divine-like mastery over other people and things. By contrast, '*imago dei* man' are human beings who ask 'who?' God is, and finding the answer in Christ, recognize that to be in *God's image* is not to ask 'how?' can I seek power and mastery, but 'who?' can I serve humbly in the image of the God of love.

Like Bonhoeffer, the 19th-century Danish philosopher and theologian, Søren Kierkegaard illustrates how strongly fideistic themes emerge when Christian theology is Christocentric:

> Reason is set aside . . . faith is not a form of knowledge; for all knowledge is either a knowledge of the Eternal . . . or it is pure historical knowledge. No knowledge can have for its object the absurdity that the Eternal is the historical.[17]

A central tenet of Christian faith is the belief that the eternal (God) becomes the historical (the man Jesus). According to Kierkegaard, belief in the incarnation, that Jesus Christ is both human and divine, is absurd, because it is an 'absolute paradox' that not only 'offends' reason but can only be believed by surrendering reason.

Now, let's say I disagree with Kierkegaard, because I don't think I have to sacrifice my reason to believe in the truth of Christianity. For example, as we shall see in Chapter 2, some philosophical theologians claim it is possible to use reason to prove God's existence logically, in the same way we prove the truths of mathematics. So, if we can know an eternal God exists as certainly as we know logic, can't I claim that at least one part of the Christian faith is believable because it is rationally provable?

Kierkegaard's response to any rational proof of an eternal God would be, so what? In Christianity, God is not just a metaphysical theory, but a physical and historical reality. The incarnation is the belief that there is a God outside space and time who breaks into space and time, an infinite divinity who became finite humanity. Any abstract theory that makes it reasonable to believe in an eternal God doesn't make it reasonable to believe that that God became flesh and blood and died on a cross in 1st-century Palestine.

So, what if I change tack, and say we can know the truth of Christianity by reasoning empirically rather than abstractly. Christians claim Jesus, a 1st-century Jewish man, was God-incarnate, despite the fact that he died on a cross. And, historical evidence shows us there was a Jewish man called Jesus, in 1st-century Palestine, who had disciples and was crucified by the Romans. So, again, can't I say that at least one part of the Christian faith seems to be feasible? Well, again, Kierkegaard's response would be, so what? Even if you know there was the historical Jesus, a finite man in the past, that doesn't prove he was also the eternal God. Also, so what if other people were his disciples then, that's not the same as saying you're his disciple now?

Kierkegaard is strongly fideistic because his point is that the Christian faith is unreasonable and must contradict rationality. It's only because Christians believe something that is radical and offends rational knowledge (God died on a cross) that they are able to do something that is extraordinary and offends reasonable behaviour (love other people to the point of self-sacrifice). It's only in sacrificing reason and the question 'How can I know?' that the real question in answer to Christ's sacrifice becomes 'Whom am I to love?'

## VIRTUE EPISTEMOLOGY

The exemplar of strong fideism for Kierkegaard is Abraham, who, in the Old Testament, is not just prepared to sacrifice reason for his belief in God, but his own son, Isaac. From a Kierkegaardian perspective, Abraham is the paradigmatic 'knight of faith': an individual who is prepared to strike out on his own, against the reasonable expectations of others, because he believes in God at the expense of all other considerations (for more on Kierkegaard's use of Abraham, see Chapter 4).

Unlike Kierkegaard, the American philosopher, Linda Zagzebski, emphasizes the communal dimensions of both faith and knowledge, and so, for that reason, I'll describe it as taking the *fides* out of *fideism*.

*Fides* is Latin for *faith*, *trust*, *loyalty*, and it was one of the foremost virtues in ancient Rome, even personified as a goddess. We inherit some of its ancient Roman meaning in the phrase *bona fides*, literally meaning *good faith*. A *bona fides* or *good faith* person is someone who always acts *bona fide* or *in good faith*, because they are persons of honesty and integrity. Consequently, it is not just that a *good faith* person always acts *in good faith* but that, as such, they can be trusted *in good faith* by other people.

Zagzebski is what is known as a virtue epistemologist. According to virtue epistemology, beliefs are not justified purely by any external evidence we can gather for them as isolated individuals (evidentialism), nor are they justified solely by how strongly we feel about them as individual knights of faith (fideism). Instead, beliefs are justified by our intellectually virtuous character.

Returning to the Roman virtue of *fides*, then, what justifies our trust in a *bona fide* or *good faith* person is their virtues. A virtue is a habit which individuals may develop, and which, once developed, becomes a feature of their character. As traits of an individual's own character, virtues inform and guide how that person behaves as true to themselves. For example, a person who has developed the virtues of courage, prudence and justice can be relied upon to act courageously, prudently and justly. A person with the virtues of *bona fides* – comprising honesty and integrity – will have traits or habits of character which mean they can be relied upon to act *bona fide* or *in good faith* in their dealings with others.

Although I am not aware of Zagzebski encapsulating her position with reference to the Roman *fides* or the terminology of *good faith*, her argument is, in effect, that we are only justified in our faith or *fides* insofar as we are intellectually virtuous or *bona fide* persons. Just as the Romans emphasized the placing of faith or trust only in *good faith* persons, so we should only place our faith or trust in beliefs we can hold *in good faith*.

Crucial here are two of Zagzebski's claims:

- 'a wide range of intellectual virtues arise out of the same *general* motivation, the motivation for knowledge, and have the same general aim, knowledge'.[18]
- 'the justifiedness of a belief . . . require[s] that he [the believer] actually holds the justified belief in a virtuous manner'.[19]

With respect to (1), the motive for knowledge is primary because this is what makes us genuine *good faith* knowledge-seekers in any subject area. If I sincerely wish to know – to have what Zagzebski also calls 'cognitive contact with reality'[20] – I will conscientiously develop the virtues, and so intellectual character, I need to pursue and to possess knowledge wherever it may be found. I will, for example, be *humble*, because I will appreciate there is much I do not know, and much I can learn from others; I will be *fair and open minded*, because I will be interested in the content of what is said, not merely who says it; I will be *courageous*, speaking out for what I take, all things considered, to be true even if it is controversial; I will be *honest*, citing the sources for my opinions when they are not entirely my own and stating as fairly and accurately as possible any opposing viewpoints; I will be *non-dogmatic* and not hold on to opinions simply because they are mine or my groups, and change my mind when I recognize the strength of an alternative viewpoint.

With respect to (2), a person with intellectual vice may think they are aiming at truth, and that their beliefs constitute knowledge; perhaps because they claim to be able to support their beliefs with reference to evidence. However, someone with intellectual vice, as opposed to intellectual virtue, does not have knowledge or justified belief, precisely because they do not pursue knowledge *in good faith*. Out of the vice of dogmatism, an intellectually vicious person may intentionally or unintentionally distort the evidence to fit their opinion, and not even fully appreciate how they are selectively choosing the evidence to support their own biased viewpoint while ignoring counterevidence. Out of the vice of idleness, an intellectually vicious person may simply adopt the opinions they hear most often from those around them, and spout the evidence cited by others in support, without checking its validity or relevance. In each case, it doesn't matter what the truth-claim of the intellectually vicious person is. The intellectually vicious and the intellectually virtuous person may agree in the beliefs that they hold; they may both hold beliefs that are widely regarded as objectively true, but only the latter is justified in believing them.

Thus, within Zagzebski's virtue epistemology, both evidentialism and fideism are incorrect. All beliefs, whether religious or non-religious, are equally a matter of *good faith*, because they are all justified on the same basis: the intellectual character of the person holding them. It is not that scientific beliefs are ultimately justified by empirical evidence and religious beliefs are ultimately justified by blind faith. Instead, we all have our beliefs about history, science, politics, religion and so on, and the justificatory test for each of them is the same: do we believe virtuously – honestly, critically, conscientiously – *in good faith* as *bona fides* persons.

Now, it is precisely because justified belief is a matter of individual virtue that Zagzebski argues beliefs are not justified individualistically, as though we can or should only look to ourselves for the beliefs that we hold. In the first place, to develop virtues we need a community of other people, teachers and exemplars, to help us learn what the virtues are, and to be schooled or trained in them: for example, to be a good student, we learn and adopt from others the best habits and practices of studiousness. In the second place, it is not only the intellectual virtues that we learn from others but many of our beliefs themselves. For Zagzebski, it can be virtuous to believe what someone else tells us to believe, insofar as we adopt the beliefs of what she calls an 'epistemic authority'. To put her position in the *good faith* language I am using here: it is virtuous to believe what someone else tells us to believe insofar as we do so *in good faith*. Only *bona fides* or *good faith* persons hold justified beliefs, but sometimes *good faith* persons are justified in the beliefs that they hold solely because they have placed their *fides* or trust in another *good faith* person.

Here, Zagzebski is aware that one criticism of Christian belief, not least within her own Roman Catholic tradition, is that people believe what they are told simply on the basis of the authority of church tradition; for example, taking their beliefs from the saints and Doctors of the Church. However, Zagzebski asks whether this is really so different from other epistemological contexts, where we also follow the guidance of experts; for example, deciding which foods it is safest to eat on the basis of health-warnings issued by government scientists.[21] Even the most virtuous knowledge-seeker cannot become an expert in everything, and sometimes what makes us intellectually virtuous is our acceptance that someone else is better placed to know more than we are. Of course, it is intellectual vice to believe government scientists out of laziness or fear, but it is intellectual virtue to follow the beliefs of the scientific community insofar as we are able to trust *in good faith* that their research has been conducted *in good faith* by *good faith* persons, sincerely seeking to have knowledge about healthy food. If it is virtuous in this context for us to trust the scientific community, then it can be virtuous to trust the church community. Again, it is intellectual vice to obey church authority out of fear or laziness, but, if your aim is to be a *good faith* pursuer of knowledge of God, it can be intellectually virtuous to submit *in good faith* to the authority of other *good faith* individuals, who have dedicated their entire lives *in good faith* to finding out about God, within a tradition of 2000 years of such individuals.

## CONCLUSION: WITTGENSTEIN AND LANGUAGE-GAMES

One way of rephrasing the question of this chapter's title *faith verses knowledge?* is to ask whether faith and knowledge are two different language-games?

The term language-game is closely associated with the 20th-century German philosopher, Ludwig Wittgenstein. What Wittgenstein meant by language-games is debated, so it is a useful way of summing up some key themes in this chapter.

Wittgenstein uses the phrases 'language-game' and 'form of life' to emphasize the fact that language is inseparable from attitudes, activities, beliefs, practices, and cultures. For Wittgenstein, 'to imagine a language means to imagine a form of life', which seems to mean we cannot imagine what we might call an inert language, a language that is isolated from the human beings who are trying to use language to interpret and to interact with each other, themselves and the world around them. Wittgenstein insists both that 'it is our acting, which lies at the bottom of the language game' and that 'This is not agreement in opinions but in form of life'. As Wittgenstein points out: 'when we come into a strange country with entirely strange traditions . . . even given a mastery of the country's language. We do not understand the people'. The meaning of words and their use, and learning what they mean and how they are used, does not come from knowing just the words themselves; it comes from knowing what Wittgenstein calls the 'whole', the activities, attitudes, forms of life of which those words are 'woven' as an inseparable part.[22]

On the question of whether faith is its own language-game, it is noteworthy that Wittgenstein gives theology as an example of how the significance of words is determined by something beneath them: 'How words are understood is not told by words alone (Theology)'. Similarly, having claimed the 'essence of language' is 'something that lies beneath the surface', Wittgenstein also writes 'Essence is expressed by grammar' and 'Theology as grammar'.[23]

For Wittgenstein, theology appears to be an example of how the words we use, and the very significance of those words, is determined, not by the words themselves, but by an often unspoken, yet fundamental, grammar or set of rules that underpin the meaning and use of words within particular language-games and forms of life. Think of the words father, bread, cross, son, wine and think of the different connotations those words have when their use is informed by Christian theology rather than in an everyday sense.

If faith is its own language-game, does that mean it is a different language-game from knowledge? Well, again, it comes back to how we define knowledge. Here, knowledge denotes theorizing about the world in ways which add to our understanding of material facts about it. To take two examples from Ayer,[24] who claimed Wittgenstein as an influence, debating the biological structure and behaviour of ants or whether there are mountains on the moon is the quest for knowledge, because it is the quest to know something about, and provable within, the world around us. Knowledge is not only just being certain of something but also being certain of something for the right reasons. So, knowledge is justified true belief, or what Wittgenstein sometimes calls 'rigorous opinions', about the world around us. Knowledge is to hold a particular view or opinion about aspects of the world on the basis of proof and justification from within the world.

As a result, there are at least two senses in which faith is not knowledge:

> First, Wittgenstein concedes that religion does not add to our knowledge, because its primary aim is not to theorize about, or to help us to understand, particular aspects of the empirical world around us. Religion doesn't help us understand things like ant behaviour and moon-mountains. Wittgenstein compares religion to ethics: it concerns questions of ultimate meaning and absolute value, the purpose of the world, life and existence, rather than discrete material facts about them.
>
> Second, faith is not knowledge, because beliefs concerning the ultimate meaning of the world are different from opinions about empirical facts within the world. As Wittgenstein observes, when

> it comes to Christian faith in the last judgement, it 'sounds queer' to say '"These people rigorously hold the opinion (or view) that there is a Last Judgement"'. Faith in the last judgement isn't an opinion or view for the believer. They aren't convinced of its truth in the same way we may be convinced of a scientific theory about ants or moon-mountains. It isn't certain knowledge of particular facts about reality, it is a certainty about the whole meaning and purpose of existence itself, it is 'utterance of belief' in something which 'culminate[s]' a whole 'form of life'. To mark the contrast between faith and knowledge, religious belief and theoretical opinion, Wittgenstein cites Kierkegaard: 'Wisdom is passionless. But faith by contrast is what Kierkegaard calls a passion' that has 'to change your life'.[25]

Wittgenstein's use of Kierkegaard suggests, like him, a fideistic division between the order of the heart and the order of the understanding, where the 'passion' of faith belongs in the first and knowledge in the second. The fideistic implications of Wittgenstein become stronger still when he questions:

> Is it 'wrong' for someone to consult an oracle rather than a physicist? 'If we call this "wrong" aren't we using our language-game as a base from which to *combat* theirs?'[26]

Here, Wittgenstein can be read as so strongly fideistic that religious faith and scientific knowledge are not only two different language-games but also language-games that necessarily compete with each other, to the extent that faith may be inaccessible to, and immune to criticism from, knowledge. Relevant to this reading is Wittgenstein's intriguing comment that 'If a lion could talk, we could not understand him'.[27] Like a lion and a human being, the physicist and the astrologist have two different forms of life, and so are playing two different language-games, with competing grammars, such that even when they use the same words they cannot understand each other.

However, while Wittgenstein's question above may serve to strengthen his fideism, it also helps to weaken it in at least two ways.

First, although Wittgenstein raises the question of whether it is 'wrong' for the language-game of physics to criticize the language-game of astrology, that doesn't mean that it *is* wrong. More importantly, it doesn't mean that the language-game of astrology is immune to criticism from other language-games (for example, in theology, sociology, psychology, anthropology) that share, or are better able to access, its grammar than the language-game of physics. Crucial here is an appreciation of Wittgenstein's definition of philosophy, and how it differs from someone like Ayer.

For Ayer and logical positivism, one function of the proper 'purpose and method of a philosophical inquiry' is to 'eliminate metaphysics'.[28] Consequently, philosophy sets limits on meaningful language and claims that a lot of the language we use, particularly in religion and ethics, is meaningless because it is not scientific, in the sense that it is not empirically verifiable. In effect, Ayer is suggesting that physics, and the sciences more broadly, are the principal language-game in town.

By contrast, Wittgenstein opposes what is sometimes called 'scientism', the view, now most famously associated with Richard Dawkins, that scientific reasoning is our only access to truth about reality. Instead, Wittgenstein is adamant that 'Philosophy is not one of the natural sciences' and that it should, in fact, set 'limits to the disputable sphere of natural science'. In Wittgenstein, philosophy does not exist to impose the scientific method and empirical verification upon all language-games as the measure of meaning, for him, 'Philosophy may in no way interfere with the actual use of language; it can in the end only describe it'.[29]

To illustrate what I take to be Wittgenstein's point here, let's take the Protestant and Catholic disagreement over whether bread and wine literally become the body and blood of Christ in the eucharist. The essence of the Protestant objection to the Catholic doctrine of transubstantiation, and the Catholic commitment to it, is religious, not scientific. It is not really a disagreement of whether the laws of physics apply to eucharistic bread and wine, and so the language-game of physics is irrelevant to understanding, accessing, entering, criticizing this disagreement. It is only theology as grammar, and not physics as grammar, that can make sense of it, and it is unphilosophical not to be interested in this difference in grammar and to conflate them.

Second, in identifying physics as a language-game, Wittgenstein's fideism is weakened because he is highlighting how the language-game of knowledge, like the language-game of faith, is underpinned by certainties that are trusted rather than known or scientifically proven.

According to Wittgenstein, 'what we do in our language-game always rests on a tacit presupposition', such that 'a language-game is only possible if one trusts something'.[30] What does a physicist trust? Well, for one thing, she trusts, like most of us, that our environment is stable and predictable. Let's return to the example of boiling water, knowing that water boils at 100°C is based on the trust that what has happened before is a stable indicator of what will happen again under the same conditions. Without the trust that the past indicates and repeats in the future, no scientific experiment could lead to knowledge, because without the trust that our environment is stable, no scientific experiment carried out in the past could justify beliefs about what will continue to happen in the future. The whole language-game of physics is built on the certainty that the past repeats, that the world will continue to behave according to predictable and measurable, unchanging and ongoing, physical laws. But the physicist doesn't *know* or try to prove the past will repeat itself – they don't know and cannot prove that water won't for some inexplicable reason just stop boiling at 100°C tomorrow even though it did yesterday – that is just something of which they, and most of us, are certain as what Wittgenstein calls an 'absolute conviction', to the extent that it would seem ridiculous to feel the need to prove it.

And so just as Wittgenstein observes it seems odd to say that faith in the last judgement is an opinion or view, he also points out that it would be odd to say I 'know' this is my left hand, or I have the 'conviction' that my body hasn't disappeared and then reappeared, or I am 'convinced that the sun is not a hole in the vault of heaven'. Like the physicist's conviction that the past is an indicator of the future, I am certain of these things, but in a way which goes beyond having knowledge of them. Knowledge is justified true belief, but my certainty or 'unshakeable conviction' in these things doesn't come from reasoning, theory and argument: 'I have not consciously arrived at the conviction by following a particular line of thought'. These convictions are just essential features of my form of life; they are already presupposed in the language-games I play.[31]

Similarly, while Wittgenstein contends that religion isn't knowledge, because it doesn't add to our understanding of the world, he also points out that it doesn't seem right to say I have knowledge that my friend is not a robot. As with belief in the last judgement for the Christian, no one is of the 'opinion' that their friend isn't a robot. An argument to prove that my friend, or any other human being, isn't a robot, even if it was successful, would not produce knowledge, because it would not 'convey any information' about the world or add to or change any absolute convictions I have. The conviction that my friend isn't a robot is already part of my fundamental 'attitude' towards him. It is a claim so obvious that it lies beyond being justified or unjustified, such that it would be absurd to try to even form an argument to prove it. It just already seems given, as part of our shared human form of life, that my friend, and all human beings I meet, are 'souls' and not robots.[32]

Consequently, it is possible to connect Wittgenstein with either or both the language of basic beliefs in Reformed epistemology and, especially, the weak fideism of Pascal's intuitions of the heart. The difference between faith and knowledge is not so simple as belief without justification verses belief with justification, because, in the end, both rely on and stem from convictions that are so fundamental or, as Wittgenstein has it, so 'anchored' and even 'animal' that it seems we 'cannot touch' them, they are just 'there – like our life'.[33] Christian belief in the last judgement, scientific belief in cause and effect and philia belief that a human is not a robot are inseparable from particular forms of life, and so within those forms of life these commitments are not knowledge or opinion, they are not justified or unjustified, reasonable or unreasonable, they are just *there* as absolute convictions, basic to the language-games played within those forms of life.

## NOTES

1 Pascal, *Pensées*, §278.
2 Schleiermacher, *Christian Faith*, §4.
3 Pascal, *Pensées*, §229.
4 Huxley, *Essays*, 350–351.
5 Huxley, 'Agnosticism: A Symposium', 4.
6 Clifford, *Ethics of Belief*, 175.
7 Ayer, *Language, Truth and Logic*, 13.
8 Ayer, *Language, Truth and Logic*, 6–7.
9 Ayer, *Langue, Truth and Logic*, 14.
10 Schleiermacher, *Christian Faith*, §5.

11 Plantinga, 'Reason and Belief in God', 66.
12 Plantinga, 'Reason and Belief in God', 66.
13 Pascal, *Pensées*, §282.
14 Kant, *Critique of Pure Reason*, A80/B106.
15 Bonhoeffer, *Christology*, 31.
16 Bonhoeffer, *Creation and Fall*, 73–74.
17 Kierkegaard, *Philosophical Fragments*, 76–77.
18 Zagzebski, *Virtues of the Mind*, 176.
19 Zagzebski, *Vairtues of the Mind*, 167.
20 Zagzebski, *Virtues of the Mind*, 243.
21 Zagzebski, *Epistemic Authority*, 112.
22 Wittgenstein, *Philosophical Investigations*, 223e, §§19, 241; *On Certainty*, §204.
23 Wittgenstein, *Zettel*, §144; *Philosophical Investigations*, §§371, 373.
24 Ayer, *Language, Truth and Logic*, 6–7; 43.
25 Wittgenstein, *Lectures and Conversations*, 57–58; *Culture and Value*, 53e.
26 Wittgenstein, *On Certainty*, §609.
27 Wittgenstein, *Philosophical Investigations*, 223e.
28 Ayer, *Language, Truth and Logic*, 13.
29 Wittgenstein, *Tractatus*, 4.111–113; *Philosophical Investigations*, §124.
30 Wittgenstein, *Philosophical Investigations*, §179; *On Certainty*, §509.
31 Wittgenstein, *On Certainty*, §101–104.
32 Wittgenstein, *Philosophical Investigations*, §178.
33 Wittgenstein, *On Certainty*, §559.

2

# GOD'S EXISTENCE

Sunday by Sunday, Christians recite the Apostles' Creed, which opens with the words, 'I believe in God the Father Almighty, Maker of heaven and earth.' This affirmation is a matter of 'faith', which can signify simply religious belief, or, more pertinently, trusting belief in God, both in his existence and attributes, such as goodness and omnipotence, none of which can be proved on the basis of empirical evidence. Let us imagine ourselves standing outside a church after a Sunday service. As the worshippers emerge, we ask them why they believe in God. Some might be puzzled, others irritated, but most would probably say it was because they have faith in God and what he has revealed to them through the Bible, their Church, and, most importantly, through the life, death and resurrection of his Son, Jesus Christ.[1]

St Paul, Christianity's first theologian, uses the example of Abraham to explain more precisely what Christian faith is. When God called Abraham, he believed God, and his faith was 'reckoned to him as righteousness'. Abraham did not doubt God's promises, nor did he ask for proof that they would be fulfilled. Rather, he grew strong in his faith because he trusted God completely. Paul draws out, for his readers, the all-important lesson they can learn from Abraham. The words about his faith being reckoned to him as righteousness were not written only for Abraham's sake, but for their sake and that of every Christian. Their faith, their trusting belief, in God, who 'raised from the dead Jesus our Lord, who was put to death for our trespasses and raised for our justification', will be counted as righteousness to them, too.[2]

DOI: 10.4324/9781003568414-3

## FAITH, REASON AND REVELATION

But is religious belief entirely a matter of faith, or is there a role for reason? Obviously, there is. The Nicene Creed contains such statements as, 'Jesus Christ, the only-begotten Son of God, Begotten of his Father before all worlds. . . . Begotten, not made, Being of one substance with the Father . . .', which require the use of reason, if they are to be understood. In his epistles, Paul discusses Christian belief in depth and detail, sometimes using complex arguments and examples, which require intellectual capacity and effort to follow. So, when it comes to Christian doctrine, reason is essential. For medieval philosophers and theologians, such as St Anselm, the originator of the ontological argument for God's existence, and St Thomas Aquinas, who put forward the most influential Christian version of the cosmological argument, the two go hand in hand. Belief in, and knowledge of, God are not achievable through unaided reason, because, in order to understand God, and that he exists, it is first necessary to believe in him. But reason is not excluded from theistic belief. As rational beings, humans have the ability to reason and to acquire knowledge through experience. For Anselm and Aquinas, reason is a gift from God to human beings, whom God has created in his own image. Thus, they both put forward philosophical arguments, which seek to show how God's existence and attributes can be established through the use of reason, and which provide a rational basis for faith.[3]

However, revelation, what God chooses to disclose of himself to human beings through, for example, prophets and holy scriptures, is the all-important source of knowledge about God. It is required to discover those truths about God which cannot be acquired through human reason. In Christianity, one example of a religious truth which is only discoverable through revelation is the doctrine of the Trinity: that God exists in three, co-equal persons, Father, Son and Holy Spirit. But, even with those religious teachings which can be known only through revelation, reason is involved in understanding and interpreting them. On the other hand, religious truths which can be discovered through reason can also be known through revelation, for if some religious truths were only discoverable through reason, knowledge of them would be restricted to an educated minority. Thus, we have 'natural' theology, what human beings can discover about God through reason and experience, and theology based on revelation. And, for Christians, grace, the help which God freely gives to human beings through Jesus Christ, which provides the means of understanding and accepting in faith what God has revealed of himself to human beings, both through holy scripture and the natural order, is also of vital importance.

## FAITH AND REASON GO HAND IN HAND

Because they seem to be very different approaches to God, we tend to dichotomize faith and reason, which would have appalled Anselm and Aquinas, as would any suggestion that their arguments should be regarded as independent, philosophical 'proofs' of God's existence, which might convince agnostics or atheists to become theists. Returning to our churchgoers, if we asked how many of them had become Christians because they had read and accepted a philosophical argument(s) for God's existence, we would be met with blank looks and a tally of zero. Anselm and Aquinas would have regarded the question as absurd. For an $11^{th}$- century monk and a 13th-century friar, their arguments would only be meaningful to those who already believe in God. And during their lifetimes, there were no atheists or agnostics to convince; medieval Europe was wholly Christian and Catholic.

Perhaps, under the influence of Kierkegaard, we also dichotomize religious faith and reason because we want to think that the former requires us to accept that God exists, even though we may have no rational or empirical basis for our belief. In making our 'leap' of faith, and committing ourselves to God, we defy reason, and almost glory in doing so. However, if we look at the Bible and the history of Christianity, we find that characterizing it as irrational or unreasonable is not an accurate representation of religious faith. In Christianity, faith does not exist in a vacuum; it is a response to a living, personal God, who is active in the world. Returning to the example of Abraham, his faith relates to his own encounters and interactions with this God, and his response to the promises that God makes to him. And because he trusts God, he always obeys God's commands. And, as Paul explains, Christian faith relates not just to God's promises but to what God has actually done through the momentous events of Jesus' life, death and resurrection. Through Jesus, in whom, 'the whole fullness of deity dwells bodily', God has intervened decisively in the world, offering human beings hope of salvation. If they listen to this Gospel or 'good news', and have faith in God and what he has done for them, they will be justified before God and will enjoy eternal life.[4]

## ST PAUL'S DESIGN ARGUMENT?

But what about those who have not yet encountered God in their lives, or never heard the Christian Gospel? How can they have faith when, as far as they are aware, there is nothing to have faith in? Despite devoting his life to spreading the Christian message of salvation, it was not St Paul's view that it was the only route to belief in God. In Romans, he foresees the 'wrath of God' being visited on those who, through 'ungodliness and wickedness', have closed their eyes to religious truth and God's existence:

> For what can be known about God is plain to them, because God has shown it to them. Ever since the creation of the world his invisible nature, namely, his eternal power and deity, has been clearly perceived in the things that have been made.[5]

This sounds like a Pauline version of the design argument for God's existence. Is Paul arguing that even those who have not heard the Christian Gospel have no excuse for lack of religious belief, because they should be able to infer God's existence from all the wonders of creation? This is a legitimate interpretation of the passage, but Paul's point is probably that, when they contemplate the natural order, even human beings who are ignorant of the Christian message should simply *see* that only God could have created it, and that it reveals 'certain aspects of His nature', such as his goodness.[6]

## DEFINITELY ARGUMENTS NOT PROOFS

Although Anselm and Aquinas did not believe that they had created standalone, philosophical 'proofs' of God's existence, some Christians have treated their arguments in this way, and some still do. However, following the devastating attacks on them by such philosophers as

David Hume, Immanuel Kant and John Stuart Mill, most Christians accept the impossibility of 'proving' God's existence and nature. The traditional arguments for God's existence, discussed in this chapter, are generally regarded as being persuasive only to those with pre-existing theistic beliefs. Their role is now seen as being what Anslem and Aquinas intended it to be: to clarify and deepen believers' understanding of God, whose existence and nature they already accept on the basis of faith.

## ONTOLOGICAL ARGUMENTS FOR GOD'S EXISTENCE

### *AN ARGUMENT IN A PRAYER*

In an earlier book, the *Monologion*, Anselm, like Aquinas in the 'Five Ways', had put forward a number of arguments for God's existence, as a 'rational basis of faith'; but he was not satisfied with this approach. He wanted a single argument, which would stand by itself, and this is what he attempts in the *Proslogion*. He thought that such an argument would be more appropriate for a God who depended on nothing else, but on whom everything else depended for its existence and well-being. It has fascinated philosophers and theologians ever since because, unlike the cosmological and design arguments, which start from human experience of the world, or interpretations of that experience, it is an *a priori* argument, which seeks to argue from God's nature or essence to his necessary existence.

The *Proslogion* is very different from a modern work of philosophy. As befits a devout monk, Anselm presents it in the form of a prayer. Though God has created him in his own image, Anselm admits that his knowledge of God has been worn down by sin. He longs to understand God, but he does not 'seek to understand in order to believe' but believes in order to understand (*credo ut intelligam*). He knows that, 'Unless I believe, I shall not understand', and seeks divine assistance, in order to understand that God is something than which 'nothing greater can be thought'.

Anselm accepts that even 'a fool', who denies God's existence, understands what is meant by something than which a greater cannot be thought. However, the existence of an object in the understanding, and understanding that the object actually exists, are very different. The fool admits that something than which a greater cannot be thought exists in the understanding, because he grasps the concept. But this concept cannot exist only in the understanding, because it can also be thought to exist 'in reality', which is greater. If that than which a greater cannot be thought exists only in the understanding, something greater than it could be thought, which is 'clearly impossible'. For Anselm, the inescapable conclusion is that something than which a greater cannot be thought exists in both the understanding and in reality.

Anselm goes on to argue that than which nothing greater can be thought exists so truly that it cannot even be thought not to exist, because something that cannot be thought not to exist is greater than something that can be thought not to exist. Therefore, it 'exists so truly that it cannot be thought not to exist'. And that than which a greater cannot be thought, and which cannot be thought not to exist, is God. Everything else that exists can be thought not to exist, because it exists less truly than God. When the fool denies God's existence, it is because he is a fool, for to understand that God is that than which a greater cannot be thought is to understand that he exists in such a way that he cannot fail to exist, even in thought.

So, God exists 'necessarily'; he is a being who cannot not-be and who cannot be thought not-to-be, whose existence, unlike everything else that exists, cannot be separated from his essential nature or essence. Anselm thanks God for helping him to understand what he had previously believed through grace. Even if he did not want to believe in God's existence, he could not now fail to understand that God exists. As the greatest being that can be thought, God alone is self-existing and created everything else 'from nothing' (*ex nihilo*), so nothing else is like God. God, the highest good, through whom everything good exists, himself lacks nothing good. He is 'whatever it is better to be than not to be'.[7]

## THE PERFECTION OF EXISTENCE AND THE NECESSARY BEING

The rationalist philosopher, Rene Descartes, begins his version of the ontological argument by wondering if there is any certainty about material things and tries to identify any distinct ideas he has about them. Even if they do not exist outside him, they cannot be regarded as nothing. For example, when he imagines a triangle, even if no such thing exists outside his thought, its 'essence' is independent of his mind. It has the property of its three angles being 'equal to two right angles', irrespective of what he may think. But, if he can derive the 'idea of something' from thought, and what he clearly and distinctly perceives as belonging to it actually does, then he can prove that God exists.

The idea of God is no less present within him than that of a triangle, and he perceives that the perfection of existence belongs to God's nature. Therefore, he should be as certain of God's existence as of any mathematical truth. However, with everything else, he can distinguish their existence from their essence, and he seems able to convince himself that this is so with God, too, and that God can be thought of as not existing. However, when he thinks carefully about the matter, he can see that it is no more possible to separate existence 'from God's essence' than to separate its having three angles equal to two right angles from the essence of a triangle. It is just as contradictory to think that God, who is 'supremely perfect', lacks the perfection of existence, as to think that the three angles of a triangle are not equal to two right angles. From the fact that he cannot think of 'God except as existing', it follows that existence is inseparable from God, and so God really exists. And, as it is to God's essence alone that 'existence belongs', there could not be more than one such God. He clearly perceives the necessity of God's having existed from, and enduring for, eternity, and that God has many other attributes which cannot be removed or changed. It is only his own prejudices and the insistent images of sensible things that make it hard for him to see that God, 'to whose essence alone existence belongs', necessarily exists.

There is a great deal in Descartes' version of the ontological argument that invites challenge, not least his claim, as a rationalist philosopher, who believes that reason, not sense experience, is the principal source of knowledge, that whatever is clear and distinct to his mind must be true. However, what is of particular interest is that, unlike Anselm, who argues that God, as the being than which a greater cannot be thought, must exist and cannot be thought not to exist, Descartes, by treating existence as a perfection or attribute which God must possess, along with omnipotence, omniscience and so on, makes his version of the ontological argument even more vulnerable to philosophical attack, as we shall see below.

Another rationalist philosopher, Gottfried Wilhelm Leibniz, maintains that the supreme substance is 'unique, universal and necessary', a pure sequence of possible being, 'incapable of limitation' and containing 'as much reality as possible'. God is 'absolutely perfect', perfection being 'the magnitude of positive reality', when all limitations have been removed. Unlike 'created things', whose perfections come from God, but whose imperfections arise from their own limited natures, God's perfection is 'absolutely infinite'. As the source of both existences and essences, God is the source of whatever is 'real in the possible'. Without God, not only would nothing exist, but nothing would even be possible. So, if there is reality, it is based on something existent and actual, a necessary being, 'in whom essence includes existence', whose possibility is 'sufficient to produce actuality'. Only God, 'the Necessary Being', has the attribute that, if he is possible, 'he must necessarily exist', for nothing is able to prevent the possibility of that which involves 'no bounds, no negation, and consequently no contradiction'.

Leibniz's argument is as breathtaking as it is brief, and he insists that 'this alone is sufficient to establish *a priori* God's existence'. We are entitled to doubt it, and we look at the damning criticisms of his and the other versions of the ontological argument below. But although he has not achieved his purpose, and proved the existence of God *a priori*, what a magnificent exposition this section of the *Monadology* is of the nature of the infinite, universal, one and only God, in whom Christians believe.[8]

## THE 'FOOL' HITS BACK

Even in the 11th century, Anselm's version of the argument did not go unchallenged. Another monk, Gaunilo, rejected the claim that a being than which nothing greater can be thought cannot be thought not to exist. Even God can be thought not to exist, so further proof was required to support Anselm's claim that God only needs to be thought of for 'the understanding to perceive with complete certainty that it undoubtedly exists'. Indeed, Anselm's argument could be used to define anything into existence. For example, it could be argued that the idea of a supposedly perfect island exists in the understanding. But, as it is 'more excellent' to exist in reality than only in the understanding, it must also exist in reality.

In response, Anselm tries to explain more fully what he meant by the idea of that than which nothing greater can be thought existing 'necessarily'. Such a being has this type of existence because, as they do not consist of parts, they cannot be thought of as beginning to exist. Only things with a 'beginning or end', and which consist of parts, or which do not exist 'always and everywhere as a whole', can be thought of as not existing. Anselm also dismisses Gaunilo's perfect island argument, on the grounds that his argument could only apply to 'that than which a greater cannot be thought', which is God. However, it seems perfectly possible to have a concept of such a being, but still to think that it does not exist.[9]

## THINGS MAY BE EVIDENT IN THEMSELVES BUT NOT TO US

Thomas Aquinas' rejects the ontological argument because it does not distinguish between things that are self-evident in themselves and also to us, and those that are self-evident in themselves but not to us. In a self-evident proposition, 'the predicate is included in the essence of the subject', as in '*Man is an animal*'; as we know the essence of both predicate and subject, the proposition is self-evident to us. However, as 'God is His own existence', subject and predicate are the same, and as we do not know 'the essence of God', the proposition '*God exists*', is not self-evident to us. If we knew God's essence, we would know that God is a being that must exist, but, as we do not, we cannot prove his existence by an *a priori* argument from the idea of God. Instead, we must turn to *a posteriori* arguments, and, starting with our own experience, argue to God's existence from the 'things that are more known to us':'His effects' – the world God has made and the things it contains.[10]

## CONFUSING LOGICAL NECESSITY WITH NECESSARY EXISTENCE

The most telling criticism of the ontological argument is Immanuel Kant's contention, in the *Critique of Pure Reason*, that it confuses logical necessity and necessary existence. If we suppose the existence of a triangle, three angles must necessarily exist in it, because having three angles is part of the definition of a triangle. It would be self-contradictory to suppose the existence of the triangle but not of its three angles. However, it is not self-contradictory to suppose the non-existence of the triangle together with its three angles. Similarly, if we form an *a priori* concept of God that includes existence, it will be self-contradictory to deny that God exists. But 'no contradiction arises' if both God and existence ('subject and predicate') are suppressed. If we eliminate its existence in thought, we eliminate the thing itself, together 'with all its predicates'. There is then no room for contradiction. If we build existence into our concept of God, it will be self-contradictory to deny God's existence, and, in this sense, God cannot be thought not to exist. But this does not prove that God actually exists.

## EXISTENCE IS NOT A PREDICATE

Kant also insists that the ontological argument is erroneous in treating existence as a perfection or predicate. Existence is not a concept of something that can be added to the concept of a thing. To say, '*God is*', adds 'no new predicate to the concept of God'. It simply affirms 'the existence of the subject [God], with all its predicates'. A hundred real pounds contains no more money than a hundred possible pounds. If they did, the concept would not correspond exactly to its object. Therefore, however many predicates something that we think of may have, we do not add another predicate to it when we add the statement that the thing we are thinking of exists. Otherwise, 'not exactly the same, but something more than what was thought in my concept, would exist'. Existence is not another (and greater) perfection or predicate that something has. To say that something exists, is to say that there exists in reality an object that corresponds to our concept. Kant likens Descartes' and Leibniz's attempts 'to increase our stock of knowledge by the aid of mere ideas', and to prove God's existence *a priori*, to a merchant trying 'to augment his wealth by the addition of noughts to his cash account'; they 'utterly failed'.[11]

## A DEEPER UNDERSTANDING OF GOD

If God exists, he exists in a completely different way from everything else, because, he is, as Anselm puts it, 'the one supreme good, utterly self-sufficient, needing nothing'. But such a being may not exist and can be thought not to exist; and there is no contradiction involved in thinking so. Norman Malcolm has argued that the significance of the ontological argument does not lie in Anselm's first proof, which uses the principle that a thing is greater if it exists than if it does not exist, and which 'rests on the false doctrine that existence is a perfection', but in the second proof, which employs the different principle that 'a thing is greater if it necessarily exists than if it does not necessarily exist'. Although it is an error to regard existence as a property of things that have contingent existence, it does not follow that it is an error to regard necessary existence as a property of God. However, acceptance of this distinction does not alter the fact that no contradiction is involved in denying God's existence, so the ontological argument would still not prove God's actual existence.

Indeed, as Kierkegaard points out, the problem with the ontological argument is the failure to recognize the difference between 'factual being and ideal being'. With factual being, it is meaningless to speak of more or less being, or necessary being. Factual existence is subject to the limitation expressed by Hamlet: to be or not to be. So, when it exists, a fly has as much being as God. Factual existence is 'wholly indifferent to any and all variations in essence': everything that exists participates in being to the same degree. But when the defenders of the ontological argument refer to God's necessary existence, they speak of being '*in the ideal sense*', of God's essence. God's being may be identical with its essence, but the difficulty is to establish God's factual existence; only then can God's ideal essence be introduced into 'the sphere' of his factual existence. But the ontological argument does not establish God's factual existence; it only explores and expounds what theists believe to be his essence. Malcolm appears to admit this point when, in discussing the relationship between the ontological argument and religious belief, he observes that it might impress its readers 'as a piece of logic', without touching them 'religiously'. And this could be (as Malcolm also acknowledges) because the argument can only be fully understood by those who are already inclined to believe in 'an infinitely great being', and who view it 'from the *inside* not just from the outside'. And that is Anselm's position: belief not only precedes understanding but also central to it. He did not expect that his argument would persuade atheists to embrace theism, or even to mean much to anyone who does not have a pre-existing belief in God. However, he did believe that it would help those who already believe in God, through faith, as he did himself, to achieve a deeper understanding of God.[12]

## COSMOLOGICAL ARGUMENTS FOR GOD'S EXISTENCE

Aquinas maintains that God's existence can be established by natural reason, but not by an *a priori* argument. He explains that there are two kinds of proof of God's existence: those (ontological arguments) that start with (the concept of) God, and those that start with God's effects. As mere creatures, with all the limitations of finite existence, human beings do not have access to God's essence, so we cannot start from God. However, we do have access to the world God has made. Therefore, we need to use *a posteriori* arguments, which start with our experience of the world, and argue from the world to God's existence. Aquinas concedes that his argument will not provide perfect knowledge of God, because effects (the finite world) and cause (infinite God) are not in proportion. But, as every effect depends upon its cause, if there is an effect, there must be a cause, so we can establish the existence of the cause: God. However, although the argument starts with the world, and is to that extent *a posteriori*, it presupposes a view of the world as contingent and dependent, something which could not-be and which requires something else beyond it to account for its existence and operation. This 'something else' is a being that cannot not-be, a necessary being: God. Only those who wonder why anything at all exists are likely to experience the world in this way. So, cosmological arguments are unlikely to convince those who do not start out with a God-centred view of the world.

## FIRST CAUSE AND FIRST MOVER

Aquinas puts forward five *a posteriori* proofs of God's existence, the 'Five Ways'. The first and second are similar, and were more convincing in an era of limited scientific knowledge, as they assume that there cannot be an infinite regress of finite causes. In the first way, Aquinas argues that some things in the world are in motion, but, as nothing can move itself, they must be moved by something else. But if this continued 'to infinity', there would be no first, or any other, mover, so there must be a first mover: God. The second way is based on causation. There is 'an order of efficient causes' in the world, but nothing can be is its own efficient cause, because to be so, it would have to be prior to itself. As to remove the cause is to remove the effect, there must be a first cause, or there would be no other causes. Proceeding to infinity would give no 'first efficient cause', and no intermediate or ultimate effects. Therefore, there must be a first efficient cause: God.

Aquinas' fifth way is a teleological argument, which is discussed below. The fourth way argues from fact that things in the world are judged to be more or less 'good', or whatever quality is being considered. But 'more' and 'less' are 'predicated of different things', to the extent that they resemble a maximum, such as the hottest, for example. The maximum in any genus is the cause of all that belongs to it, as fire causes all hot things. Therefore, there must be something, which, for all beings, causes their being, goodness, and 'every other perfection': God.

## POSSIBILITY AND NECESSITY

Aquinas' third way concerns 'possibility and necessity'. Things in nature could be or not be, so they cannot always have existed, because 'that which can not-be at some time is not'. But, if everything were of this kind, there would be a time when nothing existed. However, if that were the case, even now nothing would exist, because nothing would have 'begun to exist'. So, not all things are 'merely possible'; there must exist something that has necessary existence. The necessity of every 'necessary thing' is either caused by something else or it is not. However, as with efficient causes, it is impossible to go to infinity with necessary things, whose necessity is caused by something else, so, there must be something 'having of itself its own necessity': God. Thomists (followers of Aquinas), like the Roman Catholic philosopher, Frederick Copleston, regard Aquinas's third way, which distinguishes between finite or contingent things and an infinite, necessary being, as the fundamental one, because it contains the central idea of *a posteriori* arguments for God's existence: the 'dependence' of the world upon God. If the existence of finite being, the world, is seen as a problem, the only answer is to affirm the existence of a necessary and infinite being. Aquinas considers that his arguments show the inadequacy of any non-theistic account of the world, which attempts to show that: natural things can be explained by nature and human decisions by human reason. Both what happens in nature, and what happens as a result of human reason, must be traced back to a higher cause: a 'self-necessary first principle': God.

## A BEING CONTAINING WITHIN ITSELF THE REASON OF ITS EXISTENCE

Drawing on the third way, Copleston argues that beings in the world do not contain in themselves the reason for their existence. For example, human beings depend for their origin and existence on their parents, the air they breathe, food, and so on. The world is simply the totality of individual objects, none of which contains in itself the reason for its existence. Since objects or events exist, and no object of experience contains within itself the reason of its existence, the totality of objects must have a cause or reason external to itself. Either that cause or reason contains the reason for its own existence, or it does not. If not, the search for one that does must continue. But proceeding to infinity would not provide any explanation of the existence of anything. So, in order to explain the existence of anything at all, there must be a being which contains within itself the reason for its own existence, 'a being which is absolutely necessary (*per se necessarium*). . . . "And we call the being God"'.[13]

## A CAUSE CANNOT BE INFERIOR TO ITS EFFECT

Descartes' version of the cosmological argument is very different from Aquinas'. His concern is not with the cause of the universe, but with the cause of himself as a thinking being. He maintains that something cannot come from nothing, nor can the less perfect produce the more perfect, so his idea of God, the infinite and omnipotent creator, cannot have originated from himself. Although he has the idea of substance, he is finite, which does not account for his idea of 'infinite substance'. As this, his most clear and distinct idea, cannot be false, it must have come from an infinite substance, God. As his idea of God contains everything he recognizes as involving some perfection, he considers the possibility that, as his own knowledge might increase to infinity, he could (potentially) possess the perfections he ascribes to God himself. However, there is nothing potential in God, who is infinite and whose perfections cannot be added to, while the fact that his own knowledge still has to grow proves his own imperfection. Therefore, the idea of a being 'more perfect' than himself must come from one who actually is so. The facts of his existing, and having 'an idea of a most perfect being', prove God's existence. And, as God made him, it is all the more credible that God should have made him 'in his image'. When he thinks about himself, he recognizes his own incompleteness and dependence on a being, who possesses all the things to which he aspires.

It may seem surprising that the British, empiricist philosopher, John Locke, puts forward a version of the cosmological argument which has points in common with that of the rationalist, Descartes. However, although Locke refers to knowledge based on 'an intuitive Certainty', his argument focuses on the nature of the world, and the sort of beings it contains, rather than on his own existence as a thinking being. Locke agrees with Descartes that, '*bare nothing can no more produce any real Being*', than it can be 'equal to two right angles'. There are 'two sorts of Beings' in the world, the 'purely material' and '*incogitative*', which lack perception or thought; and perceiving, 'cogitative' beings, as we are ourselves. If there is 'something eternal', it must necessarily be a 'cogitative Being', because it is as impossible to believe that 'incogitative Matter should produce a cogitative Being, as that nothing, or the negation of all Being, should produce a positive Being or Matter'.[14]

## THE PRINCIPLE OF SUFFICIENT REASON

Leibniz holds that human reasoning is based on the two great principles of 'Contradiction', which enables us to determine what is false, and 'Sufficient Reason', which enables us to recognize that no fact can exist, or statement be true, unless there is a sufficient reason why it should be 'thus and not otherwise' – although, in general, we do not know what these reasons are. He also maintains that there are two kinds of truth, those of reasoning and those of fact. The first are 'necessary' truths, the opposites of which are impossible, as they would breach the principle of contradiction. The second, as matters of fact, are 'contingent'; their opposites are possible. This distinction suggests that the principle of sufficient reason applies to truths of reasoning, which are analytic and *a priori*, but not to factual ones, which are synthetic and *a posteriori*. But this is not Leibniz's view. The principle of sufficient reason applies to factual truths, which have a factual, if not a logical, necessity. Further, although there may be an infinite sequence of things or events, extending through the universe of created beings, there must be a 'sufficient or ultimate reason', outside the sequence of contingent events, which explains the series. This ultimate reason must be 'a necessary substance', in which all the events that will occur are present 'potentially': and this is God. Since this being is the reason for everything that occurs, has occurred, and will occur, there is only '*one God*', who is a sufficient or complete explanation of all that exists and happens.

So, although the non-occurrence of contingent events would not be self-contradictory, they cannot be other than they are, because of the factual necessity that attaches to them. There is a sufficient reason(s) for every event; if we knew the reason, we would know why it occurred, and if we knew why it occurred, we would see that it had to occur. Leibniz considers his argument for God's existence to be *a posteriori*, because it moves from (his interpretation of) the nature of the universe to God, and concludes that God must exist, because contingent beings exist, and a necessary being is the only ultimate and sufficient reason for their existence.[15]

## NO REASON TO SUPPOSE THAT THE UNIVERSE HAS A CAUSE

David Hume subjects the cosmological argument to devastating criticism. It is not an *a posteriori* argument, but an *a priori* one, because it is not based on experience, except to the extent that there is a world. Further, it depends on a particular view of the world: that it is contingent, and so its existence can only be explained if there is something that has necessary existence: God. As the cosmological argument involves necessary existence, it is vulnerable to the same kind of criticisms as the ontological argument. People may claim that God is a necessarily existent being, and, if we knew his 'whole essence or nature', we would see that it is impossible for him not to exist. However, given our limited faculties, we are not going to. But if we require something to be 'necessarily existent', why not choose the 'material universe', which we actually experience, rather than an invisible God, of whose existence we have no proof? The universe may contain qualities which, if we knew about them, would make its non-existence seem as great a contradiction as twice two being five. The argument that the world is contingent, and can be thought of as destroyed or changed, also applies to God, who can be conceived as non-existent. And there is no need for a 'first author', to explain the chain of efficient causes. In 'a succession of objects', each one is caused by the preceding one. Stating the chain of causes provides a full explanation of how each individual object came into being. It is absurd, having heard such an explanation, to ask for the single cause of the succession of objects as a whole.[16]

Bertrand Russell queries the very concept of a necessary being; 'necessary' applies only to propositions, not entities. Referring to Leibniz's division of propositions into truths of reason and truths of fact, he points out that only the truths or reason, such as 'Irrational animals are animals', are actually necessary. As they are analytic propositions, it would be self-contradictory to deny them. So, there could only be a 'necessary' being, if denying their existence would be self-contradictory. As for the concept of cause, it is derived from observation of particular things. There is no reason to suppose that the universe as a whole has any cause whatsoever; it is 'just there', and that is all that can be said. Every man who exists has a mother, and the cosmological argument seems to claim that therefore the human race must have a mother, but it obviously does not.[17]

## BACK TO THE ONTOLOGICAL ARGUMENT

Kant insists that the cosmological argument is just a route into the ontological argument. He characterizes the cosmological argument as:

> If something exists, an absolutely necessary being must likewise exist.
> Now I, at least exist.
> Consequently, there exists an absolutely necessary being.

Thus, the minor premise 'contains an experience', while the major premise argues from 'a general experience' to the existence of a necessary being. And, in order to provide an apparently 'secure foundation', the proponents of the cosmological argument profess to base 'its conclusions upon experience'. This also gives the impression that it is an *a posteriori* argument, completely distinct from the ontological argument, which relies on '*a priori* concepts'. But experience is only used to enable reason to take one step: 'to the existence of a necessary being'. However, as experience is unable to determine 'the properties' of this necessary being, it is then abandoned, and reason pursues its enquiries in 'the sphere of pure concepts', to discover, not what the properties of a necessary being actually are, but what reason decides they 'ought to be'. It finds them 'in the concept of an *ens realissimum*', a being (God) who is absolutely necessary and supremely real, and a sufficient or complete explanation of all that exists and happens.

Kant identifies the main flaw in the argument. It improperly applies the principle that everything must have a cause to ultimate reality, when it has no significance outside the empirical world or world of sense. From the impossibility of an 'infinite ascending series of causes' within the empirical world, it illegitimately infers that there is a first cause outside it. The purpose of the cosmological argument is to avoid having to prove the existence of a necessary being '*a priori* from mere concepts', as in the ontological argument. While the existence of a necessary being, who is the complete explanation of all that exists and happens, is conceivable, it is impossible to demonstrate, on the basis of experience, that such a being necessarily exists, or even exists at all. Kant has already shown that it is impossible to do so by the use of reason alone in his critique of the ontological argument.[18]

## DO WE REALLY NEED TO EXPLAIN THE EXISTENCE OF THE WORLD?

As an objective proof of God's existence, the cosmological argument does not work. Some people do not wonder why there is a universe, nor they do see it as contingent and finite. Like Russell, they think it just exists and does not need a necessary and infinite being to explain its existence. However, Frederick Copleston indicates its continuing value when he talks about seeing the existence of a finite being as a problem. The cosmological argument may help those people who do wonder why there is a universe, and who do see it as contingent, and requiring an explanation in terms of something beyond itself, to relate their perception of the nature of the world to its creator and cause: God.

## DESIGN/TELEOLOGICAL ARGUMENTS FOR THE EXISTENCE OF GOD

The design argument focuses on (what are claimed to be) similarities between the world or aspects of it, and objects which have been designed by human beings. It then argues that, as the effects are similar, so are the causes. Further, given the self-evident similarity between the world that God has made and objects made by human beings, we can infer that God resembles human beings, even though he is much more powerful. The related teleological argument argues from the apparently purposeful behaviour of even non-rational and inanimate things in the world to the existence of an intelligent being who governs it. In his fifth way, Aquinas claims that even those things in the world that lack intelligence act in a way that is clearly designed, as they move towards a *telos* or end, in order to obtain the best result. As they lack knowledge, an intelligent being, God, must direct them towards their end, just as the archer does an arrow.

Critics of the design argument point out that the similarity between the world and objects of human design is not so striking as to justify an inference to a similar cause. Not everyone sees the world as having the character of being designed; far from being a self-evident feature of the world, it indicates a particular, theistic way of looking at it. Another problem with the design or teleological argument is that, even if it worked, it would fall short of proving the existence of an all-powerful God who created the world from nothing.

## THE WORLD RESEMBLES A HUMAN ARTEFACT . . .

In Hume's *Dialogues Concerning Natural Religion*, three philosophers debate the issues of God's existence and nature, and the extent to which they can be known by means of natural reason, without the aid of revelation. Cleanthes, a champion of natural theology, puts forward a version of the design argument, while Demea, who represents an orthodox stance in religious matters, dismisses the suggestion that human beings can learn anything about God through reason. Philo represents a sceptical position. All the protagonists accept that God exists, so the focus of their debate is on the question of whether human beings can establish anything about God's existence and nature from their experience of the world. Putting forward an eloquent statement of the evidence for design in the world, 'the whole and every part' of which is 'nothing but one great machine', Cleanthes contends that the similarity between the world that God has made and human artifacts is self-evident, as the:

> adapting of means to ends, throughout all nature, resembles exactly, though it much exceeds, the productions of human contrivance; of human design, thought, wisdom and Intelligence.

By the rules of analogy, we 'are led to infer . . . that the causes also resemble' each other, although God's powers, being 'proportioned to the grandeur of the work', are much greater than ours. By means of this 'argument *a posteriori*', based on the similarity of the world God has designed to objects designed by human beings, it is possible to 'prove at once the existence of a Deity and his similarity to human mind and intelligence'.[19]

## . . . IT IS JUST LIKE A WATCH

Probably the most influential version of the design argument is put forward by William Paley. He supposes himself pitching his foot against a stone and wondering how it came to be there. It would not be absurd to think that it had been there forever. But, if he came across a watch, that answer would be unsatisfactory. Unlike a stone, a watch has parts, which have been 'put together for a purpose', that of measuring time. If the parts had been different, or differently assembled, they could not serve this purpose. Paley concludes that anyone who examines it will draw the inevitable inference that the watch 'must have had a maker', who understood how to construct a watch and designed it to serve its specific purpose.

Paley rules out possible objections to this inference. The conclusion would not be weakened if we had 'never seen a watch made' and had never known a watchmaker. Indeed, such ignorance could only increase our admiration of the unknown artificer's skill. Nor would it be weakened if the watch did not work perfectly, or there were parts whose function we could not explain. because the purpose for which it had been designed would still be obvious. The evidence of design, which exists in a watch, or any other human artefact, is paralleled in the works of nature. However, in nature, the number, variety and degree of instances of design, and of adaptation of means to ends, is much greater than in human artifacts.[20]

## WHEN DID YOU LAST SEE A WORLD BEING DESIGNED?

The sceptical Philo provides a devastating riposte to Cleanthes' arguments (and also to Paley's, which were actually written years later), pointing out that the similarity between the world and objects of human design is not as striking as Cleanthes maintains, and does not entitle us to infer similar causes. When we see a house, we know from past experience that an architect has designed it, because it is 'that species of effect which we have experienced to proceed from that species of cause'. But as we have not seen worlds being designed, we go beyond our experience, when we reach conclusions about the cause of the world, or even whether it has a cause. Philo's point is that not everyone sees the world as having the character of being designed. So far from being a self-evident feature of the world, as Cleanthes claims, it indicates a theistic way of looking at it. Further, we are not entitled to say that the world needs a cause and a designer, but God does not. And even if the analogy between the world and an object of human design is accepted, the world's many defects mean that we cannot infer, from our experience of it alone, that God is perfect. We would expect a perfect God to have designed a perfect world. Again, there is nothing about the world which tells us for sure that it was designed by only one God, rather than a number of gods working together.

True, the world operates in an orderly and predictable way, which suggests design, but, as Philo points out, unless it operated predictably, according to 'steady, inviolable laws', it would not be a stable, inhabitable environment. And there is no need to conclude that this stability must have been caused by God. A simpler explanation is that the world is governed by an 'eternal, inherent principle of order'. Cleanthes is displaying an unjustified bias in favour of the causal principle of intelligent design, as shown by his original analogy between the world and an object of human design. In fact, the world resembles an animal or a vegetable more than a machine, suggesting 'generation or vegetation' as its cause.[21]

## WE KNOW THAT HUMAN BEINGS MAKE WATCHES

John Stuart Mill finds the design argument persuasive, but not wholly convincing. It is presented as an inductive argument from the evidence of design in the world to the existence of a designer, who in certain respects resembles human beings. However, Paley's watch illustration 'puts the case much too strongly', as we already know from 'direct experience' that human beings make watches. On the basis of experience, all that we are entitled to draw is an analogy between human artifacts, which are known to be products of design, and the apparent evidence of design in nature. While the resemblances between some aspects of nature and human artifacts may provide a degree of presumption in favour of a similar cause, it is hard to say how great such a presumption is. Nevertheless, the argument is strengthened, not just by the resemblances, but by their 'special character'. Certain aspects of nature, like the eye, do seem to be designed to achieve particular ends or purposes.

So, there is evidence of some causal connection between the arrangements of nature and the ends they fulfil, and these adaptations of nature do afford a 'balance of probability in favour of creation by intelligence'. However, an 'intelligent will' is not the only possible causal connection between, for example, the eye's mechanism and the fact of sight. An alternative is the idea of the 'survival of the fittest': that those animals which, through a process of natural adaptation, developed the ability to see, survived because of their advantages over those that did not.[22]

## THE ONTOLOGICAL ARGUMENT AGAIN

Like Mill, Kant expresses respect for the design or '*physico-theological* argument', and its attempt to draw an inference from the analogy between certain 'products of nature' and 'those of human art', such as a house or watch, to the same kind of causality. Nature, like human artifacts, seems to exhibit evidence of being produced by understanding and will. And Kant accepts that it would be impossible to proceed at all, except on the basis of this analogy, because human artifacts are the only products of which we know the origin and cause. However, the adaptation of means to ends in nature, which, according to the physico-theological argument, indicates intelligent design, relates only to the form, not the substance of the natural world.

To advance further, it would be necessary to go beyond our empirical experience of the natural word, and to prove that its 'harmony and order' would be impossible, unless its '*substance*', as well as its form, were the products of 'a supreme wisdom'. As we cannot do so, the most that the proponents of the physico-theological argument could prove would be the existence of an '*architect of the world*', whose labours are limited by the material they work with, not a '*creator of the world*' from nothing (*ex nihilo*), 'to whom all things are subject'. From the presence of order and the adaptation of means to ends in the world, we can only infer (at best) a cause sufficient to produce these effects, a divine architect or crafter. However, as this is found to be unsatisfactory, the proponents of the physico-theological argument fall back on the cosmological argument and then the ontological argument, to establish 'the existence of a Supreme Being'. Kant commends them for attempting to ground an empirical proof of God's existence in human experience of the world but suggests that they should recognize their own dependence on the kind of speculative metaphysics found in the other theistic arguments:

> if they reflect upon . . . their own arguments, they will find that, after following for some time the path of nature and experience, and discovering themselves no nearer their object, they suddenly leave this path and pass into the region of pure possibility, where they hope to reach upon the wings of ideas what had eluded all their empirical investigations.[23]

Like the cosmological argument, the design argument ultimately depends on the ontological argument, and so fails as a proof of God's existence. However, (experience of) the world does suggest at least the possibility of intelligent design, so if someone is already inclined to see the world as 'designed', the design argument, as expounded by 'Cleanthes' or William Paley, may help to clarify their thinking about the relationship between God and the world, and to indicate some of God's attributes. And the results of continuing scientific research into the world's operation and origins may strengthen the perception of this possibility.

## DO THE TRADITIONAL ARGUMENTS FOR GOD'S EXISTENCE HAVE ANY VALUE?

### *THE IMPOSSIBILITY AND ABSURDITY OF TRYING TO PROVE GOD'S EXISTENCE*

The traditional philosophical and theological arguments for God's existence, though they may clarify and strengthen the theist's understanding of God and God's nature, do not work as objective proofs of God's existence. Theists may find this outcome disappointing, but the counter-arguments, particularly those of Kant and Hume, are more powerful than the arguments themselves. With characteristic insight and wit, Kierkegaard describes the whole enterprise of trying to prove the existence of God, 'this unknown something', as a 'paradoxical passion'. For 'if God does not exist, it would . . . be impossible to prove it; and if he does exist it would be folly to attempt it'. Those who try to do so will have presupposed God's existence as certain, otherwise they would not make the attempt. So far from proving anything, they merely 'develop the content of a conception'.

Their attempted proof is bound to be very different from what it purports to be, because reasoning must always move *from* existence, never *to* it. For example, no-one would try to prove the existence of Napoleon from his deeds. Although Napoleon's existence would explain the deeds, the deeds would not prove Napoleon's existence. If, at the outset, they are called Napoleon's deeds, 'the proof becomes superfluous', while it could never be proved, from the deeds themselves, that they were Napoleon's. Theists may contend that it is different with God, and that 'an absolute relationship' exists between God and his works, as only God could have created them. However, unless we assume God's existence, it is not obvious what his works are. Theists talk about God's goodness and wise governance of the world, but these are not manifest 'upon the very face of things'. What happens is that the argument proceeds from an 'ideal interpretation' of what are assumed all along to be God's works. However, as reason repeatedly collides with the unknown, 'which does indeed exist, but is unknown', it cannot advance beyond this point. The reality is that God's existence emerges, not as the conclusion of a process of reasoned argument, but 'by a leap' – of faith.

And faith concerns individuals, who, against the background of a universe that appears to lack a rational purpose, must choose their beliefs, values and way of life for themselves. Kierkegaard's choice is for God and Christianity, which he characterizes as involving a constantly reaffirmed commitment to a God, who cannot be objectively known and whose existence cannot be proved. Faith requires the suspension of reason, because it is contrary to it. In teaching that God is infinite and all-powerful, Christian faith defies reason; in teaching that, at a particular point in history, this God took on human form (became incarnate) in the person of Jesus and suffered and died on a cross for the sake of human beings, is 'absurd'.[24]

## IS RELIGIOUS BELIEF SO ABSURD AND UNREASONABLE?

It is hard to resist Kierkegaard's powerful and persuasive prose, but there is an obvious flaw in his line of argument. It does not follow, from our being unable to produce an objective proof of God's existence, that theistic belief must therefore be unreasonable and absurd, or that the arguments for God's existence are so much misspent intellectual effort. They may not work as proofs, but this does not make them valueless. As an antidote to Kierkegaard, and for guidance as to how the theistic arguments may be used to support faith, we will turn from one of Christianity's most extreme and provocative thinkers to perhaps its most rational and moderate.

Joseph Butler regrets that there is (even in the 18th century) a strong presumption against the truth of Christianity, despite its reasonableness. As Christian beliefs cannot be proved by empirical means, they are considered to be false. But the fact that something cannot be proved or completely understood, does not make it untrue. And this is the principle we apply to the empirical world, where our inability to comprehend aspects of how it operates does not lead to total scepticism: the standard we apply is that of probability, not certainty. Butler stresses this all-important distinction between probability and certainty. We develop our knowledge of the world through observation of events. We observe one event following another, infer a causal relationship between them and develop a conviction that the same pattern will be repeated. This is not the demonstrative certainty of mathematical or logical propositions; their non-occurrence would not breach the law of contradiction. Probability is about what is more likely to occur, so is a matter of degree. Butler accepts that knowledge based on probability is not entirely satisfactory, but, whereas nothing would be merely probable to an 'infinite Intelligence', like God, it is the most that finite human beings can hope for and is our 'very guide of life'. In difficult matters, such as religion, certainty is unattainable, given the inadequate nature of the evidence. Decisions must be reached on the basis of probability, even though doubt will remain.[25]

## GOING BEYOND WHAT WE SEE IN THE WORLD AROUND US

We can apply this approach to the arguments for God's existence. Theists and non-theists inhabit the same world but see it differently. Non-theists see the world as a brute fact and do not think that it needs to be explained in terms of a cause outside itself. Theists insist on going beyond the material universe, the existence of which no-one disputes, and postulate a transcendent being, God, as its cause. Religious beliefs run counter to the principle of 'Ockham's Razor', which holds that entities should not be multiplied unnecessarily, and that simpler explanations should always be preferred to more complicated ones. The theists' worldview undeniably contains a significant, additional entity, God, though they would not agree that it is an unnecessary one.

Anselm and Aquinas, Leibniz and Locke, Descartes and Paley cannot prove that this significant, additional entity exists, but do their arguments lead us to regard God's existence as more probable than not? Individuals must approach them with an open mind and decide for themselves. Butler, writing four centuries ago, in an era of intellectual ferment and scepticism, rightly deplores the widespread assumption that Christianity is fictitious. But nobody has yet produced a proof that God does not exist. Kant and Hume overmatched the proponents of the theistic arguments, but we can still learn from the philosophical and theological insights we find in these arguments. Having studied them, we may conclude, quite legitimately, that we are more convinced of God's existence than we were before, and that the reasons they give for God's existence support and strengthen religious belief.

## A RATIONAL BASIS FOR FAITH

John Hick analyses religious faith in terms of our response to the significance of different levels of human experience: the physical world, human relations and moral obligation, and the religious dimension. In order to relate to each of these levels, we must make a primary act of interpretation which, in relation to God, is called faith. This is 'not distinct from the task of directing ourselves within the natural and ethical spheres' but involves 'a way of so directing ourselves'. However, while nobody fails to appreciate the significance of the physical world, and few that of the ethical sphere, many people simply do not perceive the theistic dimension of human experience at any point during their lives.

The traditional philosophical and theological arguments may fall short as proofs of God's existence, but, working hand-in-hand with faith, as Anselm and Aquinas maintained that they must, they are important building-blocks in the construction of what Anselm called the 'rational basis', and they can help human beings to become aware of the religious aspect of human experience, to grasp its significance and to interpret the world theistically. Contrary to Kierkegaard, they also show that, so far from being absurd, religious belief is both rational and reasonable.[26]

## NOTES

1 Book of Common Prayer, 11–12.
2 Romans 4:3, 24–25.
3 Book of Common Prayer, 240–241.
4 Colossians 2:9.
5 Romans 1:18–20.
6 Baillie, *Our Knowledge of God*, 126.
7 Anselm, *Proslogion*, 93–94. 97–102.
8 Descartes, *Meditations*, 87–92; Leibniz, *Monadology*, 461–462.
9 Anselm, *Proslogion*, 121–126, 129–139.
10 Aquinas. *Basic Writings*, 19.
11 Kant, *Critique of Pure Reason,* 407–412.
12 Anselm, *Proslogion*, 113; Hick, *The Existence of God*, 51, 53, 67; Kierkegaard, *Philosophical Fragments*, 32–33.
13 Aquinas, *Basic Writings*, 18–24; Copleston, *Aquinas*, 124.
14 Descartes, *Meditations*, 75–81; Locke, *Enquiry*, 391–405.
15 Leibniz, *Monadology,* 460–461.
16 Hume, *Dialogues*, 54–57.
17 Hick, *The Existence of God*, 168–178.
18 Kant, *Critique of Pure Reason*, 412–421.
19 Hume, *Dialogues*, 13–15.
20 Paley, *Natural Theology*, 7–31.
21 Hume, *Dialogues*, 16–22, 30–33, 35–37, 39–43, 44–48.
22 Mill, *Three Essays on Religion*, 167–175.
23 Kant, *Critique of Pure Reason*, 422–427.
24 Kierkegaard, *Philosophical Fragments*, 50–55, *Fear and Trembling*, 61.
25 Butler, *Analogy*, 1–8.
26 Hick, *Faith and Knowledge*, 107; Anselm, *Proslogion*, 93.

3

# MYSTICISM AND RELIGIOUS LANGUAGE

When discussing religious language and mysticism, one of the first things to ask is whether you want to be positive or negative!?

Is this the same as asking whether you want your theology to be optimistic or pessimistic? Well, sort of, but only on a particular issue:

- Positive theology is optimism about the capacity to know God, and to speak of him directly in and through language.
- Negative theology is pessimism about the capacity to know God, and to speak of him directly in and through language.

And, as always in philosophical theology, there's a catch:

- Sometimes negative theology starts by being positive, and sometimes positive theology turns negative.

In order to understand the differences and connections between these two approaches, let's start by being positive . . .

## POSITIVE OR CATAPHATIC THEOLOGY

'Positive theology' derives from the Greek word *cataphatic* meaning 'affirmation'.

So, positive or cataphatic theology is the view that there are some things that we can actually affirm, directly and positively say, about

DOI: 10.4324/9781003568414-4

God. It's for this reason that positive theology is also termed the 'way of speech' and the 'theology of light':

- 'Way of speech', because it is insisting that there is a way of speaking about God, of affirming facts about his being and nature.
- 'Theology of light', because God can be seen, illuminated, revealed in and through the words we have to speak directly and positively about him.

## PROPOSITIONAL REVELATION

So, we're being positive: the cataphatic theologian thinks that there are words (way of speech) to illuminate (theology of light) God's being.

But, where do these words come from?

Well, one answer, which helps to bolster positive theology, is simply to say that the words we have to describe God come from God himself, so that revelation is God revealing himself to us in and through particular words. Such a view of revelation is called *propositional*.

Propositional revelation maintains that God reveals himself in and through propositions, in particular words, phrases, statements, sentences.

Now, of course, it is possible for people to disagree about how revelation is received from God, but still agree that revelation is propositional.

For example, a biblicist who believes that the Bible is literally true, was written by divine inspiration and is the only way of knowing anything about God, may hold a propositional view of revelation – but so may a hyper-rationalist or radical deist, who believes that the Bible is false and that the only legitimate source of divine revelation is human reason and not the Bible.

The deist and the biblicist disagree about how we get words from God (one through a holy text and one through our own minds), but they agree that when revelation is received it is received in the form of words, in which God reveals who he is, by telling us who he is, in and through particular propositions.

The Bible is, of course, full of propositions which seem to reveal something about God ('God is love', 'I am the way the truth and the light', 'I am the Lord your God'), and according to those who think it is possible to use reason to argue for the nature and existence of God, human reason is also full of propositions about God.

For example, Anselm famously contends that we know in our own minds that God is 'that which no greater can be thought', and from knowing that God is 'supremely great' we know he must also be 'supremely good' and 'eternal', otherwise he would not be 'supreme among all existing things' (for more on Anselm's argument for God, see Chapter 2).

Similarly, Descartes argues that God has implanted a 'clear and distinct idea' of himself in all of our minds. Although this is a revelation through an idea, it is still propositional revelation because the idea is stateable and shareable in propositions. It is through the idea of God, which we have from God, that we know him to be, and can speak of him as, all-powerful and all-good (for more on Descartes' argument for God, see Chapter 2).

The benefit of propositional revelation is that it's what we might call stable. Everyone can read the Bible and see the same words and declarative sentences written there about God. And, according to rationalists like Anselm and Descartes, there would be universal agreement that God is infinitely powerful, wise and good, if everyone would just stop and take a moment to think about God with their own reason. As Anselm puts it, any human being 'could at least convince himself of most of these things [about God] by reason alone, if he is even moderately intelligent'.[1]

## UNIVOCAL RELIGIOUS LANGUAGE

However, to be positive theologians, it's not enough just to have all these words and propositions from God. We must also know or appreciate what these words mean when applied to him. If the words (way of speech) revealed through reason or scripture do accurately reveal or illuminate God (theology of light), then whenever I speak or hear these words I must have some clear sense of how they apply to God. It's only if I know what it means to call God good, loving, powerful, and so on, that I can be confident that these words do actually refer to God and affirm something definite about him.

Consequently, if I am going to be really positive, I'll be a univocalist about religious language.

Univocal literally means one voice. So, religious language is univocal when the words we have received to speak (*vocal*) about God have one (*uni*) meaning.

If religious language is univocal and revelation is propositional, then I am justified in being an extremely positive theologian, because I can maintain that I know who and what God is through the same words that I have received from God to describe who and what he is. I have various words (love, good, wise, etc.), which I know I should be using to talk about God, because they came directly from God through reason and scripture. And, in using these God-given words to refer to God, I know not just *why* I am using them (because they came from God) but *how* I am using them (what sense or meaning they have when affirmed of God). If religious language is univocal, there is a fundamental connection between what words like love, good and wise mean when applied to God and how I normally understand them.

## NEGATIVE THEOLOGY

Now, you may have noticed that all this positivity doesn't really sound like mysticism. Mysticism suggests both mystery and the mystical, not least the mysteriousness of God and individual mystics pursuing mystical experiences in order to gain access to the divine mystery. So, positive theology, at least when religious language is univocal, doesn't seem quite like mysticism for at least two reasons.

First, if religious language is univocal, then God isn't much of a mystery, because I know who and what God is through words that describe him accurately and fully.

Second, gaining knowledge of such a knowable God is likewise not much of a mystery. Sitting down and reading the Bible or thinking about God with my own reason seem to be entirely accessible and readily available approaches to learning about God, and so are not the first things that come to mind as constituting mystical experiences or practices.

When thinking of mysticism, something more like the following is what comes to mind:

> in the earnest exercise of mystic contemplation, you leave the senses and the activities of the intellect and all things that the senses or the intellect can perceive . . . your understanding being laid to rest, you strain (so far as you may) towards a union with Him . . . neither being nor understanding can contain. For, by the unceasing and absolute renunciation of yourself and all things, you shall in pureness cast all things aside, and be released from all, and so shall be led upwards to the ray of that divine darkness which exceeds all existence.[2]

The quotation above is from a 5/6th-century author known as Pseudo-Dionysius the Areopagite, from whose works the distinction between positive and negative is principally derived.

While Pseudo-Dionysius defines positive or cataphatic theology as the theology of light and the way of speech, negative or apophatic theology is defined as the theology of darkness and the way of silence. Why this contrast?

Well, one answer lies in the example of Moses. In the Old Testament Book of Exodus, Moses climbs Mount Sinai to meet God and, in doing so, receives the 10 commandments from God directly. However, even though Moses gets physically and personally close to God, so much so it is said that he talks to God 'face to face' as a 'friend', it's also written that Moses is only allowed to see God's back, to see the person of God from behind as he passes by, because, as God tells Moses, 'you cannot see my face, because no one can see me and live'. It's for this reason that when Moses climbs Mount Sinai to encounter God he is described as approaching 'the thick darkness where God was', and when Moses asks for God's name, God gives his name as 'I am what I am' (often transliterated from the Hebrew as Yahweh or YHWH). For negative theologians it's significant that the name God gives for himself, 'I am what I am', includes no further explanation or description. Who or what is God? What is God called? How do you describe God? YHWH. I am what I am. God is God. The answer to every question about God is unanswerable directly because God just is God, I am what I am, beyond human description and comprehension, just as Psalm 18 says God 'made darkness his secret place; his pavilion round about him were dark waters and thick clouds of the skies'.

Positive theology is the theology of light and the way of speech, because it suggests at least one of two things: (1) that God can be seen to be described and (2) that descriptions of God exist that enable us to visualize who and what he is. Negative theology denies both of these points in emphasising the darkness of God. Just as Moses could not see God face to face, the darkness of God means that we can never see him directly and then find the words to describe him accurately, or in hearing and reading other people's words have a clear vision of God that adequately penetrates his darkness. Negative theology is the theology of darkness and the way of silence, because it denies both that God can be seen directly in a way which allows him to be described in words, and that it is possible to find words that allow us to visualize completely who and what God is.

However, negative theology is not just negative because it claims we can*not* describe God. Negative theology is also the claim that it is only possible, and also preferable, to focus on what God is not rather than what he is.

Negative or apophatic theology comes from the Greek word *apophatic* meaning denial. And so, apophatic theology is the claim that it is better to be negative than positive, that we get closer to God through denial or negation rather than through affirmation.

A cataphatic or positive theologian might claim we can at least know and positively say that God *is* omnipotent, that he *is* perfectly God, that he *is* a being who exists, that he *is* eternal and so on. But for a negative theologian, there are at least a couple of issues with even saying these familiar things about God.

First, as God lies in darkness, it is not clear how any words we have to refer to God, even ones we have received through revelation, actually do apply to him, so that the most we can do confidently is to say what God is not rather than what he is. If God lies in darkness, then there's no way I can see him to then describe him, or see him to verify the way I've heard him described, or see him to know in what way he is what I've heard him to be.

Second, approaching God cataphatically, by trying to know what he is, and to pretend that we can know what he is because we can use words like omnipresent and omnibenevolent to describe him, actually cuts us off from experiencing God. As God lies in darkness, and so is beyond human words, ideas and concepts that stay at the level of words always put up a barrier against a genuine encounter with God. God cannot be experienced directly in or as words and ideas, or be encountered directly through speaking and thinking. The darkness of God is beyond, and comes to us from beyond, all that we can know and say, overwhelming human language and understanding. It is only by moving beyond our attempts to know and to talk about God directly and actively that we are able to be taken up into the darkness of God silently and passively.

It is here that we can appreciate why negative theology is not just the theology of darkness but the way of silence. To experience God is to be rendered absolutely silent because it is to be overcome by the darkness of God, which is beyond words, such that we must become silent, and give up on words, if we are to leave ourselves open to receiving the darkness of God.

Of course, the question is how do we give up on words, how do we become silent so that we may experience the absolute silence of God? For Pseudo-Dionysius, the answer lies in the apophatic process of negation or denial, which he calls agnosia or unknowing.

Seriously considering what God is not encourages you to unknow what you think you know about God. When I say I know God is omnibenevolent I stop. There, I've said it. I know what God is. But, in fact, I shouldn't stop there, because I still haven't experienced God, I haven't got any further than the words and concepts I've come up with to talk about God. But what if I don't focus on what I think I know and can say about God, but focus on an absolute negation. What if I don't say, 'God is omnipotent', but 'God is a potato'!? It is a shocking and contradictory thing to say, but that's the point. Really going to the effort of thinking of God as a potato pushes me into a never-ending process of thinking about all the ways God is and is not a potato, it encourages me to unknow everything I think I definitely know and can directly say about God, pushing me towards silence, where a mystical experience of the mystery of God is possible. The process of seriously considering God as a potato won't stop unless and until I go silent, unable to do anything but wonder at the inexplicable mystery of God. And it's here, in silence, when I stop trying to approach God directly and explicably through words that I indirectly and inexplicably open up a space in myself which the mystery of God can fill:

> Unto this darkness which is beyond light we pray that we may come, and may attain unto vision through the loss of sight and knowledge, and that in the ceasing thus to see or to know we may learn to know that which is beyond or perception and understanding.[3]

## MANIFESTATIONAL REVELATION

As the 'way of silence', negative theology is bound to have consequences for propositional revelation.

Remember propositional revelation maintains that God reveals himself in and through words in a way which bolsters cataphatic or positive theology: I have words to speak about God, because they come from God, and it is these words themselves that reveal or illuminate God.

Within negative theology, God does not reveal himself in and through words, so revelation in an apophatic context is what is called non-propositional or manifestational.

When revelation is manifestational, it is not that God reveals himself through words and ideas, but rather that God manifests *himself* to us. We may use words to try to describe who or what God is as he is has manifested himself to us, but God is not revealed in, or by those words, he is revealed by what he does and in signs he gives us, rather than in words themselves.

Although negative theology emphasizes manifestational over propositional revelation, not least through individual mystical experiences of God, it is important to note you don't have to be a negative theologian to maintain that revelation is manifestational.

Negative theology maintains that God is a mystery and darkness, indescribable and unknowable, even as he is experienced. When mystics like Pseudo-Dionysius describe their experiences of God as, for example, an ecstatic silence, they are not claiming that these descriptions adequately and accurately describe God or even their experiences of him. God's manifestation of himself was non-propositional, not through words but silence, and so the experience of God's manifestation of himself is not directly shareable or stateable in words either. However, a cataphatic theologian may likewise emphasise manifestational revelation through individual religious experience but just be less negative and mystical about it. You might be really positive and claim that God has disclosed himself clearly and obviously to you through religious experience in a way you can fully describe.

Also, just as manifestational revelation doesn't mean you have to be negative, it also doesn't mean you have to view personal religious experience, mystical or otherwise, as the only or primary means by which God reveals or manifests himself to human beings. Indeed, most manifestational views of revelation are intended to emphasize the fact that the Bible is a principal source of divine revelation because it is, in fact, non-propositional and not, as discussed above, propositional.

On a manifestational view, the point about the Bible is that it reveals God, not through declarative sentences that just directly tell us what he is, but because it gives us stories and language, recounts events and experiences, that show us what God is. For example, God self-discloses himself as *creator* through Genesis 1 and 2 and the Johannie prologue, as *power* through the story of Job, and as *redeemer* through the New Testament, not because God just says 'I am redeemer, creator, unlimited power', but because scripture recounts God's showing and manifesting that he is these things. God is revealed not in or as particular words and sentences, but God is revealed because he has manifested himself, revealed who he is by what he does, and it is this self-revealing, as re-told in the Bible, that is significant rather than any particular propositions, as such.

## TERESA OF ÁVILA AND THE STAGES OF PRAYER

Just as it is important to note you don't have to be a negative theologian to maintain that revelation is manifestational, it's also important to note that there is a place for propositional revelation within negative theology.

At the beginning of this chapter, I said that negative theology sometimes starts out by being positive. What I meant by that was, for negative theologians, the way of speech is often necessary as a starting point to reach the way of silence. Consequently, it is not that negative theology has to dismiss propositional revelation, even as it emphasizes the non-propositional nature of the genuine encounter with God. The 16th-century Spanish mystic, St Teresa of Ávila, is a good example of this.

Teresa distinguishes four stages of prayer and uses the image of water to describe the journey to God along them.

The first stage is 'active recollection', where the devotee is like a gardener who is watering their garden with a bucket. The garden stands for the soul and the water is God, and just as it requires a lot of physical effort to water a garden with a bucket, so it requires a lot of physical effort to begin to prepare the soul for God. At this first stage of active recollection, Teresa emphasizes focusing on and speaking particular propositions and forms of words to begin thinking about who God is and what it is to worship him. For example, Teresa says that we may start by focusing on what we know of God by natural reason alone; for example, by observing how the beauty of nature around us reveals God as all-powerful and all-good. More particularly, Teresa emphasizes the practice of vocal prayer, saying the Lord's prayer over and over again. She admits that just saying the formal set words of the Lord's prayer from the Bible over and over again might seem, and actually become, dry and 'arid', just as it is tedious having to keep refilling and carrying a bucket of water. But, if you really go to the extreme and repetitive effort of focusing deeply on the meaning of every word of vocal prayer as you say it the water of God will begin to spill into your soul, just as the water begins to enrich your garden as your heave it from your bucket.

Gradually, after the efforts of mental prayer and active recollection, prayers, through the next two stages, become less active and more passive; less about what the individual is doing themselves and more about how God is entering into and enlivening the soul that has gone to the effort of opening itself towards God.

Along these stages prayer becomes less vocal and more 'mental prayer', which is not prayer following formal propositions already received, but inner experiences between the worshipper and God, wherein she becomes increasingly quiet as God becomes increasingly active in and for her. At these stages, God 'now takes upon Himself the gardener's work' and 'will have the soul take its ease'.[4] In other words, Teresa's imagery of the gardener illustrates how the labour of active speech prepares the way for the fulfilment of passive silence, which is release into the activities and energies of God. A gardener who has started their garden successfully with a bucket will eventually need more water for their flourishing garden, such that she will go to the effort of building a waterwheel. But now a lot of the water supplied into the garden is without her direct effort, and this increase in water makes the garden grow further, so that the gardener constructs an irrigation system, after which the garden receives even more water without the gardener's direct activity. Finally, the gardener experiences a thunderstorm, which entirely overwhelms her garden without even the gardener's indirect effort.

In other words, at each stage of the garden, as with each stage of prayer, the gardener has more water, and the soul has deeper experiences of God, but with less direct activity by the gardener or the worshipper, until they are rendered entirely passive. The final stage of prayer is, then, like the garden in the thunderstorm, where the worshipper, in silence, is utterly overwhelmed by a 'perfect union with God' which is effected by God in the soul as the 'devotion of ecstasy'. Teresa's most famous description of one such ecstatic experience of God is as follows:

> I saw in his hand a long spear of gold, and at the iron's point there seemed to be a little fire. He appeared to me to be thrusting it at times into my heart, and to pierce my very entrails; when he drew it out, he seemed to draw them out also, and to leave me all on fire with a great love of God. The pain was so great, that it made me moan; and yet so surpassing was the sweetness of this excessive pain, that I could not wish to be rid of it. The soul is satisfied now with nothing less than God.[5]

Teresa's description of the ecstatic encounter with God has remained controversial, now not least due to its sexualized language and imagery. At the time, Teresa wrote her autobiography, explaining her practice of mystical devotion and ecstatic experiences, to reassure the church authorities that she was not being deceived by the devil. However, despite being controversial, Teresa's mysticism is significant because it highlights limits in absolute separations between positive and negative theology, when her mysticism is the journey from activity into passivity, words into silence, and positivity into negativity. Accordingly, Teresa's mysticism points to limits in any absolute distinction between mysticism and rationalism, especially when, following the analysis of philosopher Christia Mercer, Teresa and the mystical tradition more broadly are a lost influence on Descartes.

As Mercer points out, Descartes' most famous book is his *Meditations*, and meditation is another word Teresa has for the first stage of prayer as active recollection. More than this, in his *Meditations*, Descartes is practicing something like Teresa's active recollection. Teresa's active recollection is a journey inwards where, to use another of her images, like a silkworm, one actively and increasingly cocoons oneself from everything else outside, travelling deeper and deeper into one's innermost self, wherein one finds God, who comforts and fulfils the soul, releasing its activity in passive fulfilment. Descartes practices what's called methodological scepticism, doubting (or we might say, returning to Pseudo-Dionysius, 'unknowing'), the reality of everything around him, the physical world, mathematical truth, the existence of other people and even the reality of his own body and past. He finds it is possible to doubt absolutely everything until he journeys increasingly inwards and finds the only thing he cannot doubt: the existence of his own thinking soul as inseparable from the idea of a perfect and loving God. Here, Descartes is also like Teresa, just as she had to convince the church authorities she was experiencing God rather the devil, in his *Meditations*, Descartes is always concerned to ensure he is not being deceived in his experiences by a demon rather than God (for more on Descartes' methodological scepticism, see Chapters 2 and 5).

## GOD: KNOWING/COMPREHENDING AND REFERRING/DESCRIBING

The comparison between Teresa and Descartes highlights how we don't have to make a sharp divide between certain kinds of rationalism and mysticism, let alone between positive and negative theology, the way of speech and silence. Indeed, at the beginning of this chapter I mentioned that just as negative theology can start out by being positive, positivity can turn negative, which is to say rationalism can drift into mysticism. Anselm is a good illustration of this.

Anselm wrote his works for his fellow monks, in the same way that Teresa wrote her books for her fellow nuns. Perhaps the two most famous aspects of Anselm's devotional and philosophical works are his ontological argument for the existence of God and his phrase 'faith seeking understanding'.

Where faith seeks understanding, it is love, devotion, belief seeking to develop a better appreciation of the object of its faith, not least by using human reason to investigate, so far as possible, the existence and nature of God. In Anselm's ontological argument (see Chapter 2), human reason knows God as the greatest that can be thought, and so that which is supreme goodness, wisdom, and power.

However, it is clear that even Anselm sets limits on what it is possible to understand, and so say, about God even as faith seeks understanding through reason:

> The mystery of so sublime a thing seems to me to transcend every power of human understanding, and for that reason I think one should refrain for attempting to explain how this is true. After all, I think someone investigating an incomprehensible thing ought to be satisfied if his reasoning arrives at the knowledge that the thing most certainly exists, even his understanding cannot fathom how it is so.[6]

According to Anselm's ontological argument, we know that God exists necessarily. But think about what it means for there to be a being in the universe who has necessary existence. It means there is only one being that exists, God, who has what is sometimes called *aseity*: a being who is independent and self-sufficient, who exists always, is uncreated, but creates everything else. With everything else we can ask why does it exist, what reason or purpose does it have? But not God. God is the reason of his own existence. God just is as he is. I am what I am. It makes no sense to ask why does God exist? God just exists, always. It might make sense to ask why did God do this or allow this to happen? But it wouldn't make sense to ask was God less or more than God when he did it? God is just God. Everything else that exits depends on God for both its actual existence and the meaning and purpose of its existence. But not God. God creates everything but depends on and needs nothing other than himself, and everything he creates is completely other to, and different from, himself. Every other being, substance, thing that exists has a beginning, if not also an end. Immortal souls and angels may live forever, but they still had to begin. Not God. God wasn't created, never begins and never ends. Unlike everything else, God is eternal, his existence is necessary, and so while he is the creator of everything that exists he is also always unique from everything else that exists.

In the quotation above, Anselm is pointing out that through reason we may know that this unique eternal substance we call God exists, but that doesn't mean we can understand how or why he exists. So, here Anselm is distinguishing between *knowing* and *comprehending* God and between *referring* to and *describing* God. The distinction is common in what is called classical theism, and so is to be found in such classical figures as Aquinas and Descartes, as we as Anselm, not least thanks to Augustine's observation, *Si comprehendus, non est Deus* ('If you understand, it is not God').

Think of the distinctions between knowing/comprehending and referring/describing in this way: I *know* that the Earth is 151.56 million kilometres from the Sun, because that's what all the latest data tells me, but I cannot *comprehend* that sort of distance in any meaningful way. I can *refer* to that distance using the words 151.56 million kilometres but that doesn't *describe* what that sort of distance is like. If I multiply my sense of what it is to travel 15 kilometres by 100 million, does that give me a sense of it? What does it mean to multiply distance by 100 million? And even if I could *comprehend* that, it wouldn't give me a sense of what it is to travel through space rather than 15 kilometres down the road. I might have this figure – 151.56 million – to name the distance, but conceiving of two objects being so far apart remains unfathomable to me. In fact, when I really think about it, it is incomprehensible to me that that reddish tiny dot in the night sky really is a whole plant, in a system of planets, within a universe full of other systems of plants, that is said to be both infinite and forever expanding. Again, there's all this *knowledge*, and all these terms to state and *refer* to what is known, but none of them helps me fully and completely encapsulate and digest, *describe* and *comprehend*, what any of this really means, and none of these words alone ever could.

It's similar to how it is with God. Through faith seeking understanding, reason gives us *knowledge* of God. We *know* that there is a God, and that he is, for example, omnibenevolent, omnipotent, omniscient, such that there are these words that we have which we can use to *refer* to this 'greatest' being that exists. But I cannot *comprehend* for a moment what it is for a being to be either omnipotent *or* omnibenevolent *or* omniscient, let alone to be omnipotent *and* omnibenevolent *and* omniscient. What does any of that really mean to me? These terms do not *describe* God, or give me a sense of what these qualities are – let alone enable me to understand what it is to be them and to possess them as this being God. All these terms help me to name and to *refer* to something I *know* is true about this being God, but even when I use these terms I'm not *describing* God, as though I can *comprehend* him; what God is fundamentally remains a mystery to me even as I use these words.

## EQUIVOCAL RELIGIOUS LANGUAGE

So, for Anselm, in encountering, and gaining knowledge of God, with and through reason, we also come up against, the very limits of human reason:

> the supreme essence is so much above and beyond every other nature that even if sometimes words are applied to him that are common to other natures, their meanings are no way common.[7]

Although Anselm may, then, be counted as a rationalist – he thinks that reason alone gives us knowledge of, and words to refer to, God – he is not a univocalist about religious language, but, in fact, takes us in a more *equivocal*, and so mystical, direction.

In univocalism about religious language, the same word when applied to God and to humans has the same meaning. So, God, in many ways, is not mysterious. If God is good, wise and powerful in a sense that I understand by those words, then I can trust, expect and predict God to act in ways I consider to be good, wise, powerful and certainly not to act in ways I would consider to be bad, silly or weak.

But in equivocalism about religious language God is mysterious, because even when we do use words to refer to him, it's still not clear – it's equivocal or ambiguous – what the same word has when applied to God as opposed to humans. So, Anselm asks in the quotation above, how can common words be used to refer to God and his creations when the supreme essence is 'so much above and beyond every other nature'?

## ANALOGICAL RELIGIOUS LANGUAGE

One answer to Anselm's question above is 'they can't'. We should just accept that all religious language is equivocal, and so avoid using it altogether, especially when it suggests the human can comprehend and describe the divine.

For example, the 12th-century Jewish philosopher, Maimonides, argued we shouldn't think of God as possessing the traditional attributes ascribed to him, and so shouldn't employ the familiar words omnibenevolent, omniscient, omnipotent, omnipresent either to describe or to refer to God. By thinking of God in terms of attributes, even these magnificent ones, we are undermining what is known as God's simplicity and unity, his oneness and uniqueness, as an essential feature of his aseity.

In effect, Maimonides point is saying that God has attributes that normalize God. Attributes are like parts of something that, when added together, comprise or make up that thing. So, if God has parts, then godness is made into something like chairness or cakeness: it is something that is made up of lots of different parts (so God is no longer simple and unified), that could be put together in lots of different ways, as though we could have various iterations of godness as we have lots of different versions of cakeness and chairness (so God is no longer unified and unique). But godness is not like chairness, cakeness or anything else at all. God is a single unique individual substance, and unique in the absolute and proper sense of that word. Often when people use the word unique they say something is really unique or very unique. That is grammatically incorrect. There are no gradations of uniqueness. Something is either unique or it's not. And this is how it is with God. God is just God. I am what I am. And because of this, if you try and talk about God in any way that corresponds to how you talk about anything else, you are undermining God's uniqueness.

So, to be negative, should we just accept that all religious language is equivocal, and avoid using it altogether, especially when it suggests the human can comprehend and describe the divine?

Well, for Aquinas, there is another option. When Anselm asks, how can common words be used to refer to God and his creations when the supreme essence is 'so much above and beyond every other nature'? Aquinas answers: *analogically*.

Aquinas proposed analogical religious language as a compromise between univocal and equivocal religious language. Why is analogy a compromise?

Well, when we speak by analogy, we say that something is *like* something else but not the *same* as something else. So, if religious language is analogical, then, when we use it, we are being both positive and negative.

Let's take the phrase 'God is good'. If religious language is analogical, then the word good here is an analogy; I am drawing an analogy between human goodness and divine goodness.

So, on the one hand, I am being positive. As an analogy, the word good does definitely and positively says something about what God is like, and so equivocalism about religious language is rejected. If we know that God's goodness is *like* human goodness, then we are able to say something meaningful about God, and, in doing so, know, for example, that God's goodness is not so ambiguous that it might turn out he is what we would call unfair or unjust.

But, at the same time, although I am being positive in rejecting equivocalism, I am also being negative in rejecting univocalism. If religious language is analogical, then when we say God is good we do not mean that God's goodness is literally the same as human goodness. The extent to which, and the sense in which, God's goodness correlates to human goodness remains mysterious. If the word good is an analogy, it might give us a sense of what God's goodness is like, but it does not and cannot *describe* God's goodness or allow us to *comprehend* it as though it is the *same* as human goodness.

The word analogy derives from the Greek word *analogia* meaning 'proportion'. So, the suggestion is that when I use such words as good, wise, powerful to refer to God I am saying God is *like* goodness, wisdom, power as I currently understand it – there is some correlation or connection between human goodness, wisdom, power, and divine goodness, wisdom, power – even if, proportionally, the latter far exceeds the former.

Think here of the phrase 'model boat'. In this context, boat is being used analogically. If you think about it, the word 'boat' here is almost absurd. In what sense is a model boat a boat in the sense that I normally understand that word when applied to a vehicle? Maybe because it's an exact replica of a particular boat? But you couldn't climb onboard the model or experience navigating the waters on her. If given a choice would you rather have a model yacht or a real one? What if a child calls a folded up bit of a paper 'a boat'? Somehow 'paper boat' makes sense analogically; this bit of a paper is somehow *like* a boat, but it is also not remotely the *same*.

Crucial to Aquinas' view is the belief that human beings are made in the image and likeness of God, and so we might say that we are, in some sense, modelled on God, which makes analogical language between humans and God possible.

According to Aquinas, 'All perfections found in creatures pre-exist in God in a more eminent way',[8] and, as humans are made in God's image, our reason (natural law) 'participates' in divine reason (eternal law). As a result, it's not that humans develop our own ideas of such perfections as goodness, power, wisdom, justice, truth and then work out how they apply to God. Instead, humans are able to use God-given reason to recognize such divine perfections as goodness, truthfulness, justice, wisdom in the world. Of course, these perfections, as they exist in an infinite God, will far exceed how we recognize and encounter them in ourselves and in a finite world. For example, when I say God is good, I realize that he must far exceed any notion of goodness I have, because he *is* goodness as infinite perfection, while I only have a finite image of what goodness is. Nonetheless, what I recognize as human goodness must somehow be modelled on divine goodness, in the same way that human beings are modelled on God. So, although human and divine goodness are different, they are still analogically connected, and so not as different as chalk and cheese, but as different as a model and a real boat.

## METAPHORICAL RELIGIOUS LANGUAGE

For negative theologians, one issue with Aquinas' attempted analogical compromise is highlighted by Kierkegaard's observation that there is an 'infinite qualitative difference'[9] between human beings and God. The implication here is that if we call God omnibenevolent, omniscient, omnipotent, or infinitely good, wise and powerful, this is not meant to denote a merely analogical or proportional difference between divine and human goodness, wisdom and power. In the same way that an infinite being is completely distinct from a finite one, infinite goodness, wisdom and power are entirely other to finite goodness, wisdom and power. There is not just a quantitative but a qualitative distinction between human beings and God, and so the difference between human perfections and divine perfections is one of quality rather than simply quantity, a difference in kind rather than just degree.

In order to respect the qualitative gap between humans and God, metaphor has been proposed as a better alternative to analogy.

- An analogy is making a literal and direct claim that two things are like each other.
- A metaphor is making a non-literal and indirect claim that two things are like each other.

So, the key difference between analogies and metaphors is that analogies are literal speech drawing a direct comparison between two things, while metaphors are a figurative and imaginative putting together of two dissimilar things in order to try to say or to illustrate something significant about one, if not both, of those things.

Let's return to the example above of model boat and take the metaphor 'a camel is the ship of the desert'. In the phrase model boat, boat seems analogical because I am saying that this other object is, in some sense, literally, like a boat: it is shaped like one, it floats, it has a mast and sail, etc. In the phrase, 'a camel is the ship of the desert', I am not saying a camel is literally like a boat or ship, so the use is metaphorical rather than analogical; the comparison works not because a camel literally looks or behaves like a boat, but because by figuratively placing together camel/ship and, by implication desert/sea, something meaningful is suggested about each.

If religious language is metaphorical, then how is this a compromise between negative and positive theology, and a different one from that of analogy?

On the negative side, metaphorical religious language is equivocal in the sense that it emphasizes that there is no way to describe or to understand God in and through words. For Janet Martin Soskice, analogies 'stretch' the meaning of words, and so religious language isn't primarily analogical because we cannot stretch our human and finite concepts and words to something divine and infinite. Consequently, religious language is principally metaphorical because, while an analogy, as soon as we use it, 'seems appropriate', with a metaphor we feel an initial 'jolt' and 'imaginative strain' in working out why certain images, words, ideas have been placed together.[10] Sallie McFague stresses the jolt from metaphorical language in famously strong terms when stating 'theology is fiction'. All the words and language we have to talk about God are created by human beings; none of it directly, knowingly or confidently encapsulates who God is. As a result, the point of a metaphor is that, unlike an analogy, it always stresses that the object being discussed is 'both like and unlike' that to which it is being compared, because:

> a metaphor is seeing one thing as something else, pretending 'this' is 'that' because we do not know how to think or talk about 'this,' so we use 'that' as a way of saying something about it.[11]

For McFague, 'father' is now a 'dead metaphor' for God because it has become so ingrained people no longer appreciate that it is a metaphor and think of it as a description. As a metaphor, God as father makes us think about parenthood and care as aspects of God, but, as a description, it makes us think that God actually is male reinforcing patriarchy.[12]

On the positive side, as Soskice points out, metaphors are like analogies in that they are the point at which negative and positive theology meet, operating within the distinction discussed above in Anselm between knowing/comprehending and referring to/describing God. If we are speaking metaphorically, then we have not gone absolutely silent; we are still employing the way of speech to say and to reveal something about God and our experiences of him. Admittedly, unlike an analogy, a metaphor is not 'straightforward speech'. It is not the attempt to reveal or to know God by saying that he is literally and directly like something else. However, that doesn't stop a metaphor from actually saying something meaningful and apt about God by having what Soskice calls 'cognitive content'. Metaphors are not empty or random. There is a difference between good and bad metaphors, because they work by the 'interanimation' of ideas as conjured and represented by words. As such, there are good and bad metaphors because it matters which words, and so which associations those words convey, are placed together.

Earlier, I used the example of 'God is a potato' as a negation of God. Well, God is also not literally a stone or a male parent, but there seems to be a difference between saying 'God is a rock' or 'father' and 'God is a potato'. Similarly, think of lots of other examples in scripture and the mystical tradition more broadly, where God is said to be something he clearly is not, but where what God said to be doesn't seem to function as a negation of God. In scripture, we hear that God is a water fountain, shepherd, mother hen, vine, bread, gate, bridegroom. In Pseudo-Dionysius, God is 'absolute ecstasy in all purity' and a 'super-essential ray' of 'darkness'. In Teresa, God is our 'companion and true friend' who is 'exceeding sweet' and the 'greatest of pains'.

When I hear that God is these things, I don't think that he is literally like them (analogical), let alone the same as them (univocal). Indeed, I may be initially shocked and confused by a lot of this language.

When I read, for example, in Julian of Norwich that 'God is mother' or in Teresa that 'God is exquisite pain', I am jolted, perhaps because I am used to the language of father and peacefulness when it comes to God, and/or because I am not sure how to reconcile these two images with each other, let alone with God. But then, when I think of the ideas and feelings that come with Julian's metaphors (of comfort, nurturance, birth, steadfastness, care), and then think of Teresa's metaphors, and the idea, of not being hurt exactly, but of being overwhelmed, of being taken into a place to be consumed absolutely beyond self, and maybe to be reborn, then I do get a sense of how they, and of how I might following them, experience, conceptualize and speak of God.

Undoubtedly, all this metaphorical religious language comes with a certain ambiguity, but perhaps that's because God is ultimately ambiguous to human beings, and so it's only by speaking metaphorically that we can meaningfully fill out or gesture towards God when we're unable to comprehend or to speak about him directly or precisely.

## CONCLUSION: 'GOD IS GOOD': UNIVOCAL, ANALOGICAL, EQUIVOCAL, METAPHORICAL?

In reviewing themes explored in this chapter, it is useful to focus on the phrase 'God is good'. Should we understand this phrase univocally, equivocally, analogically or metaphorically?

In answering this question, let's consider the following from a 17th-century French bishop and mystic, François Fénelon, who argued 'We would love' God 'as much, though by an impossible supposition he' 'would render eternally unhappy those who had loved him'.[13]

Fénelon's statement caused a great deal of controversy when it was first published, and we can see why from both a univocal and analogical perspective.

A univocalist would reject Fénelon's supposition because, when she calls God 'good', and indeed reads in the Bible that 'God is love', she takes it that 'good' and 'love' in a divine context must be the same as in a human context. If God is good and love, then God will greet those who have loved him with goodness and lovingness rather than with what sounds like, at best, indifference, and, at worst, unfairness and meanness.

Similarly, while an analogicalist doesn't think that 'good' and 'love' can or must be precisely the same when applied to God as applied to humans, she will still expect there to be a proportional relationship between divine and human goodness and lovingness, in which the divine is infinitely greater than the human. Analogically, 'God is good' means that God cannot be a source of unhappiness for those that love him, not least because God has promised heavenly reward for those that love him. If God's goodness and lovingness are like, but proportionally greater, than human goodness and lovingness, not only will God keep a promise made, he will exceed it in the reward of infinite happiness, rather than punish with its opposite, an eternal unhappiness.

By contrast, an equivocalist may point to Fénelon's statement as consistent with the fact that, although we call God 'good' and 'love', we can have no idea what these terms mean when applied to the darkness of God, and so it might be better not to try and talk about him directly at all. When it comes to human goodness and love, we may expect things like justice, care, happiness and reward in response to devotion, but these are human words, concepts and expectations that cannot be applied effectively or meaningfully to God at all.

Metaphorically speaking, Fénelon's supposition highlights how, even when we seem to be talking about God directly and literally, we are talking about him indirectly and figuratively. 'Good' when applied to God is just as metaphorical as saying 'God is a rock'. So, to follow someone like McFague, it must be the case that God both is, and is not, 'good' as we currently understand it, and appreciating that helps to shift in important ways our conception of both 'God' and 'goodness'. Understood metaphorically, 'God is good' means, following Fénelon, that in loving God as perfect goodness we are loving something entirely *other* that completely overwhelms our self and any ordinary understanding of goodness that we have. In loving the perfect mystery of God, one is taken beyond any sense of self, let alone self-reward, such that one becomes capable of loving in a divine-like way, where goodness is no longer justice, reciprocation and pleasure, but selflessness and Christ-like suffering service.

Of course, the response to equivocal and metaphorical readings of 'God is good', from an analogical and univocal perspective, is that they make religious language unstable. Fénelon may illustrate how God is magnificently and incomprehensibly beyond current human conception and values, but, in doing so, he finds it possible to speak of God in a heterodox fashion, as a cruel promise-breaker, which even he realizes is an 'impossible supposition'. McFague also turns to what, in Christianity, has long been regarded as unorthodox pantheistic language, figuratively describing the world as God's body, and birthed by Mother God, to press for the use of metaphors that make environmentalism central to Christian ethics.

Whatever one makes of the weaknesses and advantages of any of these forms of religious language, it is important to remember that it is not necessarily a straightforward either/or. As Soskice points out, it's not as though even Aquinas thought that *all* religious language is analogical, not least because analogical religious language tends to be more abstract than devotional. For Soskice, a proponent of metaphorical language may agree that when we say God is omniscient, omnipotent, omnibenevolent and so on, we are speaking analogically, but the fact is that we want to say more about God than just these technical terms. In this way, we may be convinced, analogically, that 'God is good', but find ourselves speaking metaphorically when trying to explain what God's goodness is and means.

## NOTES

1 Anselm, *Monologion*, 10.
2 Pseudo-Dionysius, *Mystical Theology*, 191–192 (I have modernised some of the spelling and grammar).
3 Pseudo-Dionysius, *Mystical Theology*, 194.
4 Teresa, *Life*, 128.
5 Teresa, *Life*, 256.
6 Anselm, *Monologion*, 77.
7 Anselm, *Monologion*, 78.
8 Aquinas, *Summa Theologiae*, I, Q.4, A.2.
9 Kierkegaard, *Sickness unto Death*, 207.
10 Soskice, *Metaphor and Religious Language*, 64–66.
11 McFague, *Metaphorical* Theology, 15–18.
12 McFague, *Metaphorical* Theology, 9, 38–41.
13 Fénelon, *Maxims*, 6.

# 4

# RELIGIOUS EXPERIENCE AND RELIGIOUS ETHICS

What is (a) religious experience? We have talked about John Hick's analysis of faith as the response to, and interpretation of, the significance of the religious dimension of human experience. Although theists and non-theists occupy the same world, they interpret it differently. Theists see themselves as God's creatures, inhabiting the world God created, and they look forward to eternal life with God at the end of their lives on earth. Let us call this religious outlook, which pervades every aspect of theists' lives, including (see below) its ethical dimension, 'experiencing the world religiously'. However, we also talk about particular 'religious experiences', possibly dramatic events, which not all religious people have. These may be extraordinary encounters with God, such as those of Moses at the burning bush, Saul of Tarsus on the road to Damascus and Jesus' disciples on the Day of Pentecost, which change a person's whole outlook on life, perhaps by turning an agnostic or atheist into an active believer. Let us call these events, which may be experienced individually or collectively, 'having a religious experience'.

Some theists may be sceptical about such experiences. Simply to dismiss them would be to cast doubt on the truth of narratives in Holy Scripture, but accepting the truth of religious experiences described in the Bible, or which have occurred in the history of a particular Christian Church, does not mean that Christians will believe every claim about religious experiences. They will test any claims against the criteria of their plausibility and reasonableness, and probably only give credence to those that have occurred within

DOI: 10.4324/9781003568414-5

the Christian tradition, and which reflect Christan teaching and ethical values.

## A REALITY WHICH TRANSCENDS THE SELF

Frederick Copleston defines a religious experience as an:

> awareness of some object which irresistibly seems to the experiencer as something transcending the self . . . of the reality of which doubt is impossible – at least during the experience.

Religious experiences are not strict proofs of God's existence, and Copleston does not rule out subjectivist explanations, especially when the experiences exhibit little connection with the lives of experiencers, or if the experiencers are known to be deluded or subject to hallucinations. But with such people as Francis of Assisi, the experience produces an 'overflow of dynamic and creative love', which can only be explained by 'the actual existence of an objective cause of the experience'. Evidence of the beneficial effects of such experiences should create a 'presumption in favour' of their objective reality, even if is not (strictly) proof of their genuineness.[1]

## THE NUMINOUS

Rudolf Otto sought to identify and describe the distinctive character of religious experiences. He found that they involve a 'feeling of dependence', or 'creature consciousness', on the part of those having them. They experience the 'emotion of a creature, submerged and overwhelmed by its own nothingness in contrast to that which is supreme above all creatures'. But this sense of dependence, and of being overwhelmed, must not be regarded as purely subjective, as 'a category of *self*-valuation, in the sense of self-depreciation'. This creature-feeling is a 'subjective concomitant and effect' of the experiencer's response to an 'object outside the self', which is holy, and therefore worthy of devotion and worship. However, Otto is not satisfied with the word 'holy', because what is '"extra" in the meaning of "holy" above and beyond the meaning of goodness' must be defined. He adopts the Latin word, '*numen*' ('the numinous': the divine) for it. A religious experience involves both a 'unique "numinous" category of value' and a '"numinous" state of mind' on the part of the experiencer:

> For the 'creature-feeling' and the sense of dependence to arise in the mind the 'numen' must be experienced as present . . . as in the case of Abraham.

Otto describes the mental state of those who experience the numinous as 'irreducible to any other'; like 'every absolutely primary and elementary datum', the numinous feeling cannot be strictly defined.

Otto refers to a numinous 'feeling', and it is not always clear whether he is referring to the experience or its object. One suggestion is that Otto should always have used 'the alternative phrase "*the feeling of the numinous*"'. It may be 'that aspect of the deity which transcends or eludes comprehension in rational or ethical terms', but the numinous is 'an objective reality, not merely a subjective feeling in the mind'. However, while the holy object of a religious experience is distinct from the experiencer, there cannot be a religious experience without an experiencer, because the experiencer's response to the divine reality, the wholly other, is always involved.[2]

## A PRAGMATIC APPROACH TO RELIGIOUS EXPERIENCE

As a philosophical pragmatist, William James thought that one of human beings' most useful ideas is the belief that, beyond or behind the empirical world, there is (some form of) ultimate reality to which they belong, and that they are happier and more fulfilled, if they believe in it:

> we have a right to believe the physical order to be only a partial order . . . we have a right to supplement it by an unseen spiritual order which we assume on trust, if only thereby life may seem to us better worth living.

As a psychologist, he was interested in the feelings and experiences of individual human beings, in so far as (they believe that) they are related to something divine: ultimate reality or God. He found that religious experiences like conversion, as well as affording the experiencer a sense of 'being wrought on by a higher control', frequently have such positive effects as producing a 'new level of spiritual vitality' and a conviction that 'impossible things have become possible'. Whether or not they are accompanied by such phenomena as visions, these experiences may engender 'a sense of astonished happiness' and a feeling in the subject that they have been 'born anew'. James also makes the important point that possible 'natural' or psychological explanations of such occurrences are not grounds for dismissing them; they must be judged by their results:

> Our spiritual judgment . . . our opinion of the significance and value of a human event or condition, must be decided on empirical grounds exclusively. If the *fruits for life* are good, we ought to idealize and venerate it.[3]

## A PRESUMPTION OF AUTHENTICITY

Richard Swinburne challenges the widely held philosophical position that an experience is 'evidence for nothing beyond itself', regarding it as a principle of rationality that, if a subject believes that something is present, it probably is. As with ordinary perceptions, religious experiences are 'substantial grounds' for believing in the reality of what is experienced, such as God or the Virgin Mary. Unless there are good reasons for doubt, there should be a presumption, which Swinburne terms the 'Principle of Credulity', in favour of regarding experiencers' reports as genuine. Swinburne proposes this principle as an antidote to the general view that it is perfectly legitimate to regard something as what it appears to be, without inductive justification, unless the supposed object of the experience lacks such qualities as colour, shape and solidity. Because they lack these sensible qualities, religious experiences are always treated with unwarranted scepticism.[4]

## CAN WE DETERMINE THE GENUINENESS OF RELIGIOUS EXPERIENCES?

So, do some people actually have religious experiences? If so, how do we differentiate between the genuine and the bogus? In describing and analysing their characteristics, Copleston, Otto, James and Swinburne have indicated some of the criteria against which we might test purported religious experiences. Otto and Copleston have focused on the numinous aspect of religious experience, as involving the experiencer's awareness of a transcendent being, which is an external, objective reality, not a product of the experiencer's beliefs or wishes; which is supreme over the experiencer and worthy of devotion and worship; and which engenders in the experiencer a sense of nothingness and complete, creaturely dependence. Copleston and James stress the point that religious experiences often produce positive, generous and self-sacrificing attitudes and conduct in the experiencer, and may be life-transforming. However, any beneficial effects on the experiencer must be regarded with caution. They may be grounds for taking a purported religious experience seriously, but they do not prove that a supreme being is its source. Swinburne argues convincingly for our approaching the issue of religious experiences with at least an open mind, rather than being sceptical to the point of disbelief and dismissal. Armed with these insights, we will now look at the three well-known biblical instances of religious experience mentioned above.

## ENCOUNTERING GOD IN A BURNING BUSH AND JESUS ON THE ROAD TO DAMASCUS

Having fled from Egypt, in fear for his life, leaving the people of Israel behind as slaves, Moses looks after the flock of his father-in-law, Jethro, the priest of Midian. As he leads his flock towards Horeb, the mountain of God, we are told that he comes across a bush, which, though burning, is not consumed by the flames. At first, Moses seems to regard the spectacle as a purely natural phenomenon and stops to gaze at it. But then God calls to Moses from the burning bush, telling him that he is the God of Abraham, Isaac and Jacob, and to remove his shoes, as he is standing on 'holy ground'. Moses hides his face, afraid to look at God, who tells Moses that he must return to Egypt, in order to end the oppression and suffering of God's people, and to lead them out of Egypt to a land which God will give them. Initially, Moses resists God's command, on the grounds that the people of Israel will not listen to him but finally agrees after the assurance that God will 'stretch out my hand and smite Egypt', forcing Pharaoh to release the people of Israel from slavery.

We first encounter Saul of Tarsus as a zealous Pharisee, a bitter opponent of Christianity and, in his own words, a 'persecutor of the church'. As the Acts of the Apostles vividly expresses it, 'breathing threats and murder against the disciples of the Lord', he obtained the high priest's authority to hunt down Christians in the Damascus synagogues. However, as he approaches the city, a heavenly light flashes around him. Flinging himself to the ground, he hears Jesus' voice calling him by name, and asking him, 'why do you persecute me?'. Those travelling with him are speechless with amazement: they hear the voice telling Saul to go into Damascus and wait to be told what to do, but can see nothing. Blinded by the vision, Saul cannot see for three days, until Ananias, a member of the Christian church in Damascus, is instructed to visit him and restore his sight – which Ananias is reluctant to do, because of Saul's fearsome reputation as a persecutor. However, he agrees to do so, when Saul's future role as missionary to the Gentiles is explained to him. After Ananias has laid hands on him, Saul is filled with the Holy Spirit, his sight returns, and he is baptized. He then enters the synagogues, not to persecute any Christians he finds there, but to proclaim Jesus as the Son of God.

What should we make of Moses' and Saul's experiences? Let us start with some of the characteristics of religious experience identified earlier. In both cases, there is ample evidence of the numinous quality Otto stresses and the presence of a transcendent being, to whom the only possible response is devotion, worship and obedience. Despite his initial feeling that the burning bush was a curiosity of nature, Moses quickly realizes that he is standing on holy ground and that God is addressing him. Saul is so shaken by his experience that he loses his sight for three days. What about the key test of the extent to which their experiences had a life-changing and beneficial effect on them? Moses realizes that he cannot evade his mission as his people's liberator any longer: he leads the Israelites out of bondage in Egypt and is the instrument of their receiving God's Law, the Ten Commandments.

William James is right to say that, for Saul, his experience marks 'a complete division . . . in the twinkling of an eye between the old life and the new'. From being the indefatigable persecutor of the

Christian community, Saul becomes Paul, its most successful missionary, taking the Christian message to the Gentiles, and laying the foundations of the worldwide Christian Church. As Christianity's first theologian, he gives the life, death and resurrection of Jesus, and his gospel of repentance and *agape*-love, a robust and enduring, doctrinal structure. But were these experiences actually of an objective reality, independent of Moses' and Saul's minds? Or did they project the inner, mental and emotional turmoil of their life-changing decision-making outwards to God? Such an interpretation is possible. There seem to have been no witnesses to Moses' experience, and his companions only partially witnessed Paul's. We must answer this question for ourselves, always keeping in mind Swinburne's principle of credulity.[5]

## INSPIRED AND EMPOWERED BY THE HOLY SPIRIT

Following his resurrection, Jesus promises his apostles that they 'shall receive power' when they have been 'baptized with the Holy Spirit'. After his ascension, on the day of the Feast of Pentecost, they hear a sound 'from heaven like a rush of a mighty wind', and see 'tongues as of fire', which rest upon each of them. Full of the Holy Spirit, they express their extraordinary spiritual experience and sense of empowerment in 'other tongues, as the Spirit gave them utterance'. Jews from across the Roman Empire have gathered in Jerusalem for the festival and are astonished to hear Jesus' Galilean disciples speaking in different languages. Some are awe-struck, but others accuse the disciples of being drunk. Peter assures the crowd that they are not and then expounds the Gospel to them. Jesus of Nazareth, having been crucified in accordance with God's 'plan and foreknowledge' and 'raised up' by God, thus conquering death, now sits at God's right hand. He has poured out the Holy Spirit on his disciples, the results of which they are seeing for themselves. The impact of Peter's words is immediate. Some three thousand people accept Peter's call to, 'Repent, and be baptized . . . in the name of Jesus Christ for the forgiveness of your sins'. The new converts then join the fellowship of a Christian community, which is based on common ownership, the eucharist and prayer.

The opening chapters of the Acts of the Apostles give a vivid account of a series of collective religious experiences, which lay the foundations of the Christian Church and its successful missionary activity. First, the apostles experience the risen Jesus, who, so far from being dead and buried, appears to them many times. He has conquered death, and now he promises them the power of the Holy Spirit to enable them to carry on his work. Then, we have the extraordinary events of the day of Pentecost, when the disciples, inspired by the Holy Spirit, go out and preach the Gospel of Christ crucified and risen to the large crowds who have gathered for the festival. They make many converts, creating a dynamic Christian community, which will preach its message of salvation far and wide. There are points that require clarification. Jesus' 'Ascension' suggests physical ascent into heaven. Allowance has to be made for a pre-scientific understanding of heaven as a physical location above the earth. The key point, as Peter explains to the crowd at Pentecost, is that Jesus, God-incarnate, is no longer with them on earth but is now, in some sense, 'exalted at the right hand of God'. Again, there is the claim that the disciples spoke an array of foreign languages, which seems improbable but no reason to accuse them of drunkenness. In fact, the reference is to unintelligible utterances, which, in the exuberance of their empowerment by the Holy Spirit, the disciples are driven to shout out. This 'glossolalia', or 'speaking in tongues', a sign of spiritual inspiration, was a common occurrence among the early Christians, and we find St Paul reproving the church at Corinth, for preferring it to more useful activities: 'He who prophesies is greater than he who speaks in tongues, unless someone interprets, so that the church may be edified'.

Did the events of the day of Pentecost happen exactly as described in the Acts of the Apostles? Perhaps not, but there can be no doubt that a series of extraordinary religious experiences occurred, which were shared and witnessed by huge numbers of people, and so cannot be dismissed as the fancy or delusion of an individual. And as with the experiences of Moses and Saul, the establishment of the Christian Church, as a vibrant and flourishing community, propagating the Gospel across the Roman Empire, testifies to the beneficial and transformational effects of these experiences. As we will see in Chapter 5, the ever-sceptical David Hume proposes that reports of miracles should not be accepted unless their non-occurrence is less probable than their occurrence. Let us apply a similar test to the religious experiences discussed above. Which is more probable: that the subsequent work and achievements of Moses, Paul and the apostles were the result of actual and life-changing encounters with God, or happened despite the fact that what they thought were genuine religious experiences were merely mistakes or delusions.[6]

## YOU DREAMT THAT GOD SPOKE TO YOU

But both collective and individual religious experiences are vulnerable to sceptical attack. With biting wit, Thomas Hobbes subjects them to the test of what we might call, 'the principle of incredulity'. If God speaks to someone, he does so directly, or through an intermediary. Someone receiving a direct communication from God will recognize and understand it, but 'how the same should be understood by another, is hard, if not impossible to know', because the recipient of the purported experience cannot produce proof of its genuineness. If someone asserts that God spoke to him in a dream, that only means they, 'dreamed that God spake to him':

> though God Almighty can speak to a man, by Dreams, Visions, Voice, and Inspiration; yet he obliges no man to beleeve [sic] he hath so done to him that pretends it; who (being a man), may err, and (which is more) may lie.

Hobbes is sceptical about any occurrence of genuine religious experience, but his main concern is probably to discourage their use as evidence of God's existence or nature. They are subjective experiences, which can be explained in natural terms, and only tell us about the experiencer's state of mind.[7]

## NO REAL EVIDENCE THAT GOD CAUSED IT

Bertrand Russell expresses (more politely) the same view as Hobbes: 'the whole argument from our mental states to something outside us, is a very tricky affair'. He points to accounts of people, 'who believe that they've heard Satan speaking to them', which sound like the reports of religious people who claim that God speaks to them. He does not think that a more valid argument can be made from the mental experiences of religious people to God's existence than from the mental experiences of those who claim to experience Satan to Satan's existence. An experience's 'good moral effect', even if it is life-changing, is not evidence that it has an external source, such as God.[8]

Alasdair MacIntyre focuses on the questionable legitimacy of any inferential step from human experiences to God. A purely mental experience could not provide 'information about anything other than the experience' itself, and even with visions or voices, there remains the insuperable problem of justifying an inferential step from what is experienced to God as its source. Such an inferential step is not comparable to one made within the empirical world, for example from smoke to a fire as its cause. An inferential step from, say, a vision to God involves a move from the empirical world, where the vision is experienced, to God as its super-empirical cause, but 'we can only infer the unseen from the seen when we have a rule of inference that entitles us to do so'. Inferential steps from effect(s) to cause are only warranted where there is a known correlation between the effect (for example, smoke) and its source (a fire). However, in the case of visions or voices, only the effect is known. There is no knowledge of God as the source of religious experiences, as there is with fire as the source of smoke. MacIntyre also makes a similar point to Hume's in relation to miracles (see Chapter 5). Even if conclusions about God could be legitimately inferred from such experiences as visions or voices, the inferences would be to conflicting religious belief systems, as the experiences relate to the religion of the experiencers' culture or society.[9]

## WHY ARE WE INSTINCTIVELY SCEPTICAL ABOUT THE AUTHENTICITY OF RELIGIOUS EXPERIENCES?

We certainly are sceptical: unless an occurrence can be pigeonholed under a general scientific law, we automatically doubt it. Every report of a supposedly supernatural experience provokes a flurry of desperate efforts to find a 'natural' explanation. And sceptics can argue that many Christians have never had life-transforming, religious experiences like those of Moses, Saul and Jesus' apostles. For the majority of Christians, their religious faith originates in their awareness (which may develop gradually) of a religious dimension to life, coupled with acceptance of their Church's teachings – though they may regard the prayer and worship in which they participate there as a form of collective or community religious experience. Moses' and Paul's experiences were essentially individual ones, and lend themselves to being characterized as fanciful or erroneous. The apostles' experience was a corporate one, ultimately involving numerous people, but it can still be dismissed as illusory or delusory. The apostles wanted to receive the gift of the Holy Spirit, and convinced themselves and each other that they had received it, while the crowd allowed themselves to be caught up in the excitement generated by the apostles' claims, and succumbed to mass hysteria and credulity.

Such a position is defensible and raises questions which make it hard to use religious experience as objective evidence of God's existence. However, sceptics should at least try to be open-minded and willing to ask themselves which is the more probable: that the experiences we have looked at were genuine, or that they are fictions or figments of wishful or delusional thinking. And they should give serious consideration to William James' test of whether what is claimed to be a religious experience has beneficial or harmful effects. In the examples we have looked at, the effects were both remarkable – and positively life-transforming,

## RELIGIOUS AND CHRISTIAN ETHICS – WHAT IS THE RELATIONSHIP BETWEEN GOD AND MORALITY?

Belief in a transcendent, omnipotent and omniscient God, who created the universe *ex nihilo*, is bound to have a major impact on what Christians regard as right or wrong and on their conduct. Kierkegaard maintains that the believer's relationship to God is absolute, taking precedence over other obligations, including generally accepted ethical principles. Certainly, the logic of the belief that God is all-knowing is that, even if his commands overturn conventional ethical principles, there must be a good reason, which human beings do not understand. However, many religious people accept that morality is independent of God's will and that God has given human beings reason and freedom, so they must take responsibility for their ethical principles, decisions and actions.

An important factor in Christian ethics is the belief that God is personal and all-loving, and cares about individual human beings. Christians believe that through Jesus, who was human but who embodied and revealed in his life on earth God's infinite love for human beings, God brought about human beings' salvation. They believe that they should follow the example of Jesus, who spent his life on earth helping others, and lead lives which reflect God's *agape* or love for them. They also regard Jesus' ethical teachings as a blueprint for living their lives ethically and religiously. Many Christians also believe that God has an ultimate purpose for them, that physical death will be followed by eternal life and that God will judge them on the basis of how they have led their lives on earth.

## THE EUTHYPHRO DILEMMA

We may be God's creatures, but if we are also, as Christians believe, rational beings, capable of judging moral issues for ourselves, with the freedom to act on our judgements, should we not decide for ourselves what is good or bad, right or wrong, and not simply obey God's commands without demur? Plato explores the question of whether or not something is good or right just because God (or the gods) wills it, through the example of a religious zealot, Euthyphro, who is about to prosecute his father for unintentionally causing the death of a day-labourer. Euthyphro defines what is good or right as what the gods love. But Socrates gets Euthyphro to see the difference between a thing being loved and its being lovable. To say a thing is loved means that someone loves it, but this is not their reason for loving it. The gods do not love good or right (holy) things because such things are in a state of being loved by them, but because they are good or right, and so lovable or worthy of being loved: 'the holy is loved because it is holy, not holy because it is loved'.

Therefore, holiness, goodness and rightness cannot be equated with, or defined in terms of, being loved or willed by the gods – or by God. Plato shows that, logically, ethical standards are distinct from, and independent of, God's will. Indeed, any attempt to define 'good' or 'right' in terms of what God loves or wills would be to commit a 'supernaturalistic' form of what G.E. Moore called the 'naturalistic fallacy'. This is the attempt to define 'good' or 'right' in terms of such natural properties as pleasure or happiness, which is what, in Moore's view, the utilitarian philosophers, Jeremy Bentham and John Stuart Mill, tried to do. The consequence is the same: moral terms are robbed of their evaluative force. It means that to ask if God loves, or wills, what is good, would only be to ask if God loves, or wills, what God loves or wills. It would not then be an 'open question' whether what God loves, or wills, is good or right, but clearly this question can be asked intelligibly. Of course, this logical distinction, between what is good and right and what God wills, does not prevent many religious people believing that, as a matter of fact, what God wills actually *is* always good or right, but it should encourage them to question whether it really is.[10]

## GOD'S COMMANDS ARE LAW . . .

However, some religious believers insist that, as God is the omnipotent and omniscient creator of the world, we should do what he tells us, even if we do not agree with or understand it. The Roman Catholic philosopher, Elizabeth Anscombe, has argued that, even in modern secular society, discussion of ethical issues reflects a history of religious belief. When used in a moral context, terms like 'ought' and 'must' have the sense of our being obliged by law to act in a particular way. What she calls this '*law* conception of ethics' comes from the Christian tradition, in which ethical rules are regarded as divine commands. In Christianity, breaking ethical rules involves disobeying God and is associated with guilt and fear of divine punishment. Therefore, talking about what we 'morally ought' to do makes no sense in a secular society, in which people no longer believe in God and so do not fear the sanction of divine punishment if they break moral rules which God has ordered them to obey.[11]

## . . . SO, WE MUST FOLLOW ABRAHAM'S EXAMPLE AND ALWAYS OBEY THEM

Kierkegaard uses the story of Abraham to explore the implications of belief in God for how we should make ethical decisions.

Abraham is an exemplar of faith because he is prepared to sacrifice his only son, Isaac, at God's command: he knew that 'no sacrifice was too hard when God demanded it'. Obeying God takes precedence over everything else, including abiding by the universal ethical principle that murder is wrong. Kierkegaard accuses religious people of double standards. As Christians, they profess to admire Abraham's faith and willingness to obey God. However, as upright members of their communities, they would probably treat a modern Abraham as criminal or insane. The Abraham story highlights the dilemma confronting religious people, who may have to decide whether to follow a universal ethical rule or obey God. By choosing the latter, Abraham showed that the individual is capable of an absolute relationship with God, higher than universal ethical principles, which can be set aside to serve the higher purpose of obeying God:

> The story of Abraham contains, then, a teleological suspension of the ethical. As the single individual he became higher than the universal. This is the paradox that cannot be mediated.

However, those who follow Abraham's example are unpopular because they challenge the moral principles and rules which govern modern society.

## A TERRIFYING RESPONSIBILITY

But if they are mistaken about what God has commanded, then persons of faith are simply moral outcasts. This possibility of error reinforces the case for always following universal ethics principles/rules, such as those prohibiting murder. And even if it could be established beyond doubt that God commanded murder, surely God should be defied, not obeyed. However, by confronting religious believers with a stark choice between obeying God, whatever his demands, or conforming to universal ethical principles, Kierkegaard challenges them to explore the full implications of belief in an omnipotent God. If they think that the whole of morality is comprised in society's 'universal' ethical principles and precepts, is there any space left for God? Does he not become 'an invisible vanishing point, an impotent thought'? Elizabeth Anscombe has highlighted the point that many religious people regard the ethical rules of their religion as laws, which God has laid down, and that to break them is to disobey God. Kierkegaard emphasizes the idea and significance of 'sin', which suggests an obligation to God above and beyond the duty to obey universal ethical principles. Sin is about individual disobedience of God; an 'ethics that ignores sin is an altogether futile discipline'.

The obvious response to Kierkegaard is to point out that the all-loving God, about whom Jesus taught, would never command actions that breached fundamental ethical principles, and that sin arises, when, by breaching universal ethical principles, such as the prohibition of murder, we also defy God, who is the originator of them. For Christians, to live ethically is to live religiously, because the Christian ethical life is inseparable from the universal moral rules that God has laid down for his human creatures to follow. And Kierkegaard himself admits the problem of people deciding for themselves that God has commanded them to flout generally-accepted ethical precepts:

> if faith is taken away . . . all that remains is the brutal fact that Abraham intended to murder Isaac, which is easy enough for anyone to imitate who does not have faith.

To read Kierkegaard is to be torn between admiration for his genius and the feeling that he took a perverse pleasure in drawing highly individualistic, but mistaken, conclusions from his reading of the Bible. The lesson of the Abraham story is not that Abraham decided to sacrifice his son in obedience to God, but that he realized, before it was too late, that it would be wholly wrong to do so and that the God in whom he believed would never command him to commit such a moral outrage. The fundamental principles of Christian ethics are to be found in the Bible; they have been incorporated into the moral rules and the laws of Christian societies and are the basis of Western civilization. The problem for Christians is not, as Kierkegaard avers, that obedience to God may require them to breach these universal ethical principles, which are drawn from Christian ethical teaching, but the concern that the mores of present-day society diverge further and further from them.[12]

## THE BIBLICAL BASIS OF CHRISTIAN ETHICS – CREATION AND THE TEN COMMANDMENTS

The Book of Genesis makes clear the absolute distinction between creator and creation. Unlike God, who is infinite and does not depend on anything else for his existence, the universe is finite and dependent. However, human beings have a special status in the created order. God made them in his own image, as rational beings and responsible stewards of his creation. According to the Book of Exodus, God gave the Ten Commandments to Moses during the people of Israel's journey from Egypt to the Promised Land. The moral rules they prescribe are the basis of any civilized society, whether religious or secular. They stipulate respect for life ('You shall not kill') and property; affirm the importance of honesty and integrity in relations with others; and lay down rules dealing with sexual relationships, the lust and avarice that lead to sexual immorality and crime, and children's obligations to their parents.

However, the duty to God takes precedence over the duty to other human beings. The Israelites must not worship 'other gods', or take God's name 'in vain', and they must set aside a day to worship him, because it was God who freed them from slavery in Egypt. So, the basis of the duty to observe the Ten Commandments is not (primarily) their benefit to human beings, but the obligation to God. They are part of God's covenant (agreement) with the Israelites, who will enjoy a special relationship with him as long as they keep his laws. There is a sensible realism about this overriding duty to God, which Christianity has inherited. Finite and fallible, they are more likely to be moral and law-abiding, and to build a civilized society, if they are also God-fearing. So, in a way, Kierkegaard is right: the priority is to obey God – but by carrying out the universal ethical rules set out in the Ten Commandments, not in following delusory commands which violate them.[13]

## AN ALL-LOVING GOD

Christianity teaches that God is all-loving, and showed his love for human beings, by being incarnated in the historical figure of Jesus Christ. Through Jesus' teaching, death and resurrection, God made salvation available to all. For Archbishop William Temple, this is Christianity's central declaration:

> No object is sufficient for the love of God short of *the world* itself. Christianity is not one more religion of individual salvation. . . . It is the one and only religion of world-redemption.

However, redemption and eternal life require human beings' faith and the practice of love. Those who believe in Jesus, and reflect God's love in their own lives, will be saved. Those who do not are 'condemned already', because they have 'not believed in the name of the only Son of God'. But what does it mean to say that Jesus was 'God-incarnate'? According to the Nicene Creed, Jesus was of the 'same substance' as God. However, many Christians find such language dated and unhelpful, especially in the context of Christian morality. John Hick distinguishes between God's metaphysical attributes, such as omnipotence and omniscience, and God's moral attributes, such as goodness and love. In the compassion Jesus showed for the sick and spiritually ignorant, Christians can see, 'what is meant by assertions such as "God is good" and "God loves his human creatures"'.[14]

## WHAT IS *AGAPE*-LOVE?

The First Letter of John declares that 'if God so loved us, we also ought to love one another'. God's love is not ordinary human love, but *agape*-love, the unlimited and self-sacrificing love that Jesus showed in his life. It does not depend on the desirableness of its object, or on such special obligations as those to family, friends or nation. *Agape*-love is unconditional and universal, extending to all human beings, because they are also God's creatures and therefore our neighbours. Its essence is expressed in Jesus' teaching about the greatest commandment:

> you shall love . . . God with all your heart, and with all your soul, and with all your mind, and with all your strength. . . . You shall love your neighbour as yourself.

Love of the neighbour derives from love of God, and Jesus uses the Parable of the Good Samaritan to explain that everyone is our neighbour, including our enemies. It is a Samaritan, regarded by Jews as an outcast and sinner, who treats the wounded robbery-victim as a neighbour; Jesus' followers must do the same and show love to everyone. He is also telling the lawyer who asked, 'Who is my neighbour?' that he put the wrong question. It should have been, 'To whom can I be a neighbour?' The answer is, 'To anyone whose need constitutes a claim on my love'.[15]

## DID JESUS EXPECT HIS ETHICAL TEACHING TO BE TAKEN LITERALLY?

The Sermon on the Mount spells out what Christian belief means for human conduct, by contrasting the Old Law, given by Moses, with Jesus' New Law, which sets more exacting ethical standards. Jesus condemns not only killing but also the motive of anger, which drives people to violence and murder. Christians must try to achieve reconciliation with those who oppose them and are forbidden from taking revenge, resisting aggression or even insisting on their rights. Jesus teaches his followers not to limit their love; it must reflect God's unconditional and indiscriminate love for all human beings. They must forgive others for the wrongs they have done, because they expect God to forgive their wrongdoing, and according to the 'Golden Rule', they must treat others as they would wish to be treated themselves.[16]

Jesus' ethical teaching in the Sermon on the Mount has been interpreted in different ways. Some claim that it should be taken at face value and applied by Christians in their everyday lives; others that it is an ultimate ideal, against which the limitations of sinful human beings are to be measured. The Russian novelist and social reformer, Leo Tolstoy, held that, through his New Law, Jesus was offering the blueprint for a kingdom of God upon earth, which would be achieved by taking Jesus' commands in the Sermon on the Mount literally and putting them into practice in their entirety, including non-resistance to violence and the rejection of law courts and punishments. He condemned the hypocrisy of political and religious leaders, who did nothing to change a society that was 'founded on principles that Jesus reproved; we do not wish to understand his doctrine in its simple and direct acceptation'. However, while Tolstoy's vision of an earthly utopia, based on non-violence and the abolition of oppressive state institutions, seems inspiring and influenced political leaders and reformers like Mahatma Gandhi, his interpretation of the Sermon on the Mount turns it into a secular creed, in which God appears to play no part.[17]

## *KERYGMA* PRECEDES *DIDACHE*

Joachim Jeremias explains that the early Christian Church had two forms of preaching: *kerygma* and *didache*. *Kerygma* was the proclamation that Jesus had redeemed human beings through his death and resurrection. This was followed by *didache* or ethical teaching, which instructed Christians about how to lead their lives. Thus, the ethical teaching in the Sermon on the Mount was not presented to Christians as a set of rules they must follow without assistance, because it was preceded by the message of salvation, which announced God's love and the forgiveness of sins. Only by beginning with the greatness of God's gifts can the heavy nature of Jesus' demands be understood. Nor is the Sermon on the Mount a complete ethical programme, covering every ethical issue that arises, or a series of rigid regulations that Christians must follow to the letter; rather, its teachings and examples indicate how Christians, conscious of salvation and of God's forgiveness, should lead their lives: 'the Sermon on the Mount is not law, but gospel'.

## CHEAP GRACE AND COSTLY GRACE

Dietrich Bonhoeffer's distinction between cheap grace and costly grace leaves no doubt about the exacting nature of the ethical demands placed on Christians. Through Jesus' death, God has given human beings grace or unmerited help to enable them to achieve salvation. However, as religious faith means obeying God, and accepting the sacrifices and suffering that this involves, grace is costly:

> It is costly because it costs a man his life . . . it is grace because it gives a man the only true life. It is costly because it condemns sin, and grace because it justifies the sinner . . . it is *costly* because it cost God the life of his Son.

Some Christians make the mistake of thinking that, because of Jesus' redemptive work, grace is cheap. They are mistaken. Jesus' ethical teaching in the Sermon on the Mount is not a list of ideals to aim at but a set of commands for Christians to obey. They can expect to be hated, persecuted and killed, as Jesus was. And, this was Bonhoeffer's experience, as he was executed by the Nazis for opposing Hitler.

## THE UNCOMPROMISING LOVE ETHIC

For Reinhold Niebuhr, the Sermon on the Mount does not give detailed guidance about how we should lead our everyday lives. What Jesus puts forward is an uncompromising love ethic, which human beings are incapable of putting into practice in their present, sinful condition:

> The ethical demands made by Jesus are incapable of fulfilment in the present existence of man. They proceed from a transcendent and divine unity of essential reality, and their final fulfilment is possible only when God transmutes the present chaos of the world into its final unity.

It is an ultimate ideal, against which the shortcomings of conventional ethical standards can be measured. It highlights the limitations of what human beings can achieve, which may lead them to 'repentance . . . the gateway to grace'.[18]

## AN ETHIC BASED ON GOD'S LOVE FOR HUMAN BEINGS

These different interpretations of Jesus' ethical teaching indicate that following it is not a straightforward matter. Are human beings capable of leading an agapeistic life, despite their sinful condition? If the Sermon on the Mount is prescribing a blueprint for everyday living, how is it to be followed in practice? *Agape*-love is said to be unconditional and universal, but it is debatable whether it is possible to love, as distinct from being concerned about, people we do not know. Love seems to relate to specific individuals, who are important to us, such as family and friends. It can also take those trying to practise it in different directions. The situational ethicist, Joseph Fletcher, argued that we should respect society's 'ethical maxims' but also be 'prepared in any situation to . . . set them aside *in the situation* if love seems better served by doing so'. However, the most loving action in a particular situation is not always obvious, nor is it always clear how we should prioritize the needs of potential recipients.[19]

But even Christians who regard Jesus' ethical teaching as too demanding for human beings to put into practice, in every detail, here and now, accept that it establishes a standard, against which they and others can measure their principles and actions, and an ethical ideal to which they can aspire. And, as Jesus explains in his teaching about the greatest commandments, Christian ethics and a purely secular moral code have different starting points. Whereas secular morality is based on human beings' respect for and responsibilities towards others, Christian ethics is based on God's love of human beings and their love of God – which means that Christians are not expected to practise *agape*-love without the assistance of God's grace.

## ARGUING FROM MORALITY TO GOD

### *THE GOD-GIVEN FACULTY OF CONSCIENCE*

In Chapter 2, we noted the difference between revealed theology and natural theology; the ethical teaching in the Bible is revealed morality. But is there an ethical equivalent to natural theology? Christianity teaches that God made human beings in his own image, so do they have a natural faculty, which disposes them towards good moral conduct, and which, like the appearance of design in the world, can be adduced as an argument for the existence of a God who implanted it? Joseph Butler argues that human conscience is this a God-given faculty, which is designed to control our passions and appetites, so that we are as well-adapted to 'moral government' as a watch is to measuring time. Conscience draws us towards good moral conduct, and, when we defer to its authority, we affirm our true nature as rational beings and autonomous, moral agents, capable of fulfilling our obligations to God. Butler accepts that human beings often fail to be guided by conscience, but yielding to our strongest passions only causes moral disharmony within ourselves.

We want to be happy, but, as finite beings, we cannot know which of our actions will produce happiness. God also wants his human creatures to be happy, and gave us a conscience, because he foreknew that our obeying it 'would produce more happiness'.[20]

John Henry Newman goes further, claiming that, through conscience, human beings can gain an image of God and give a genuine assent to the proposition that God exists. Conscience appeals to something outside itself, and is like an inner voice, which orders and constrains. Thus, we feel fearful and guilty when behaving badly, even though there are no witnesses to our misdemeanours, and we may even benefit from our immorality. Conscience, and our desire for its approval, involves recognition of God, to whom we feel accountable. In the voice of conscience, human beings sense a personal relationship with God and an awareness of God's nature, to which they respond emotionally, personally and positively. It teaches us:

> not only that God is, but what He is; it provides for the mind a real image of Him, as a medium of worship; it gives us a rule of right and wrong, as being His rule, and a code of moral duties.

Frederick Copleston maintains that the issue of moral obligation points clearly to God's existence. Most human beings distinguish between right and wrong, and are aware of a sense of 'obligation in the moral sphere'. This awareness of a moral law, imposing moral obligations to other people, is best explained on the basis that it has an 'author', God, the 'transcendent ground' of moral values.[21]

## GOD AS A POSTULATE OF THE PRACTICAL REASON

In the *Groundwork of the Metaphysics of Morals*, Immanuel Kant argues that, although there is no proof that human beings have moral freedom or freewill, without it there can be no morality, as human beings could not be held responsible for their actions. Freedom is therefore a necessary condition or postulate of practical reason (reason when it considers matters of morality), which must be presupposed in order to make sense of morality. In the *Critique of Practical Reason*, Kant argues that, in addition to freedom, God and immortality are also postulates of the practical reason. As we have previously encountered Kant as a severe critic of philosophical arguments for God's existence, it may seem surprising to find him putting forward what sounds like one himself, especially when he also insists that the moral law is independent of God.

However, postulating God's existence does not mean that morality depends on God, or that the moral law should be obeyed to please God; it is to be obeyed for its own sake. Kant's point is that human beings have an idea of the highest good, in which obeying the moral law for its own sake is rewarded by proportionate happiness. However, this term is ambiguous; it can mean the supreme good or the complete good. While virtue, being worthy of happiness, through obeying the moral law for its own sake, is the supreme good, the complete good requires happiness, too. But virtuous people do not always receive the happiness of which they are worthy. Only an all-powerful God is capable of ensuring that, ultimately, they do:

> it must lead to the presupposition . . . of a cause adequate to this effect . . . it must postulate the *existence of God*.

Immortality gives human beings the opportunity to achieve moral perfection and to receive the happiness which they deserve.

For Kant, Christian teaching brings together the ideas of the supreme good and the complete good. It teaches that the moral law should be obeyed, not to please God, but solely for its own sake. However, this leads its followers to regard the duties required by the moral law also as divine commands. God's ultimate purpose in creating the world was so that human beings could achieve the highest good. Therefore, nothing 'glorifies God more' than human beings, who are ends in themselves and have absolute worth, obeying the moral law for its own sake, and this being, 'supplemented by his splendid provision to crown such a beautiful order with commensurate happiness'.

In *Religion within the Boundaries of Mere Reason*, Kant interprets Jesus' life and death in a way that fits in with his moral system. Jesus represents the idea of a morally perfect human being whom human beings must emulate. For Kant, religion simply is morality, as there is no other service that God requires from human beings except exemplary moral conduct and obeying the moral law:

> Apart from a good life-conduct, anything which the human being supposes that he can do to become well-pleasing to God is mere religious delusion and counterfeit service of God.[22]

## BUT DO WE NEED GOD AS THE GROUND OF MORAL VALUE . . .

Bertrand Russell rejects any type of moral argument for God's existence. Some people believe that they have a moral duty to perform acts of violence, so it is difficult to regard moral obligation as having 'a Divine origin', or as evidence of God's existence; it can be accounted for in other ways. Russell, an adherent of ethical intuitionism, maintains that he distinguishes between good and bad simply by seeing the difference between them, just as he does between blue and yellow. This is not a very convincing, non-theistic account of the basis of moral values and precepts. In the context of the relationship between religion and morality, it would be better to say that theists and non-theists have (a) different, fundamental moral principle(s). Theists base their moral values on the Ten Commandments and Jesus' teaching in the Sermon on the Mount, non-theists on, for example, the utilitarian principle, that 'actions are 'right in proportion as they tend to promote happiness', or on the Kantian one: '*So act that you use humanity . . . always . . . as an end, never merely as a means*' – which has much in common with Jesus 'Golden Rule'. However, Russell is right to say that God is not the only source of fundamental moral principles.[23]

## . . . TO EXPLAIN THE EXISTENCE OF HUMAN CONSCIENCE . . .

Joseph Butler insists that conscience, which comes from God, discloses a universal law of shared moral values. As well as ascribing moral potential to all human beings, this suggests pursuit of common, God-given moral goals. In practice, human beings do not do so. Indeed, different human beings appeal to their consciences to support the adoption of very different sets of moral values and to justify pursuit of very different (and conflicting) courses of action. Being a God-given faculty is not the only explanation for the origin of conscience. It can be viewed as a natural faculty which has no connection with God; a socially conditioned response to departures from, or compliance with, the generally accepted ethical norms of society; or a metaphor for describing people's feelings of guilt or self-approbation.

Newman's analysis of conscience suggests that it gives human beings a sense of something beyond themselves. This may be psychologically accurate but does not establish God's existence. Guilt about immoral acts may come, not from God, but from our social upbringing or our psycho-physical nature. Nor does Newman's analysis account for the diversity of religions and moral codes that human beings accept through conscience. If only one God speaks to us through conscience, this suggests that we misunderstand or misinterpret what he says. And Newman does not offer us any criterion for distinguishing erroneous feelings of conscience from those that are authentically the voice of God.

## . . . OR AS A POSTULATE OF THE PRACTICAL REASON?

In the *Groundwork*, Kant stresses the independence of morality, arguing that the moral law must be obeyed for its own sake and not because of inclination or for personal advantage. However, in the *Critique of Practical Reason*, he links morality to happiness and also maintains that God is a necessary postulate of the practical reason, which seems to contradict what he says in the *Groundwork*. He is not saying that people should be moral in order to receive the reward of happiness, or that they should obey the moral law in order to please God. However, it is easy to interpret what he says in this way. Kant argues that those who obey the moral law deserve to be happy, but, as this does not always happen in this world, God and immortality must be postulated, in order that those who are virtuous can receive the happiness they deserve in the end. Kant postulates God, in order to make sense of morality, but it is perfectly possible to practise Kantian morality (as many people do) without having any belief in God or any thought of immortality or ultimate happiness.

## MORALITY MAY NOT DEPEND ON GOD . . .

For most theists, the relationship between religion and morality is obvious – morality and moral awareness depend on religion. The foundation of what is good or right lies in the will of God, and if human beings are open to God's influence and obey his commands, they will be morally good and act rightly, which are key elements in living their lives religiously. However, as a matter of logic, morality is independent of religion. It is always an open question whether what God commands is good or right, and to define 'good' or 'right' in terms of God's will or commands is to commit a supernaturalistic fallacy.

As well as these theoretical objections to the link between God and morality, there are also those that we can observe for ourselves. Many atheists and agnostics have high moral standards and treat other people with respect and compassion, while some people, who claim to be religious, do not seem to know the difference between right or wrong and behave selfishly and uncaringly towards others. As with the arguments for the existence of God that we considered in Chapter 2, the moral argument does not provide a proof of God's existence, which would compel an atheist or agnostic to believe in God: postulating God as the ground or origin of morality is more likely to be meaningful to the theist than the non theist.

## . . . BUT BELIEF IN GOD ADDS ANOTHER DIMENSION TO MORALITY

G.J. Warnock highlights the way in which theistic belief gives a different perspective on morality. It is bound to have a major impact on the believer's attitude to ethical questions, particularly in a monotheistic religion, like Christianity, which holds that God is neither all-too-human (an infinitely powerful creator) nor utterly non-human (all-loving and concerned about human beings). Secular morality has no parallel to a transcendent being who is 'uniquely an object of both love and fear . . . to whose behests is owed, uniquely, *obedience*'. Even if morality is regarded as logically independent of God, and, for agnostics and atheists, grounded in human needs, not a divine will, for religious believers, the rules of conduct that God has laid down are divine commands, involving, if disobeyed, not just breaches of ethical principles, condemned by society, but possibly (eternally) punishable sins against God. Perhaps, therefore, Damaris Masham is right in her assertion that belief in

> a Superior, Omnipotent Being, inspecting our Actions, and who will Reward or Punish us accordingly . . . is in all Men's Apprehensions . . . the only stable and irresistible Argument for submitting our Desires to a constant Regulation, wherein it is that Vertue does consist.

Without God, there is a sense in which anything is permitted. However, once God comes into the picture, there really are moral imperatives.[24]

In view of Christianity's emphasis on the importance of leading an agapeistic life, T.E. Jessop makes the interesting point that there is no formal Christian ethical creed, setting out Christian moral values and duties. He suggests the 'hymn of love', from I Corinthians 13, in which St Paul declares that, 'If I speak in the tongues of men and of angels, but have not love, I am a noisy gong or a clanging cymbal', and explores the meaning of Christian love as, 'patient and kind . . . not jealous or boastful . . . not irritable or resentful', which 'rejoices in the right . . . bears all things, believes all things, hopes all things, endures all things. Love never ends'. Recited Sunday by Sunday, like the Apostles' and Nicene Creeds, it would bring home the 'practical truth . . . that Christlike love is even in us immortal'.[25]

Arguments such as those of Butler, Newman and Copleston will carry limited weight with non-believers, who will demand objective evidence that God is the ground of moral values, or that conscience is a God-given faculty. For the theist, however, these arguments will relate to their actual experience of God, and of God as a source of moral imperatives, which religious belief requires them to obey. And non-believers may see in the attitude of (some) theists towards moral issues, in their treatment of moral principles as moral imperatives originating in God's will, and the way in which they lead their lives religiously, in strict accordance with these divine moral imperatives, what can become a form of moral argument for the existence of God.

## NOTES

1 Hick, *The Existence of God*, 178–182.
2 Otto, *The Idea of the Holy*, 5–11, xvi–xvii.
3 James, *The Will to Believe*, 22; *The Varieties of Religious Experience*, 31, 236–241.
4 Swinburne, *The Existence of God*, 254.
5 Exodus 3:1–22; Philippians 3:6; Acts 9:1–30; James, *The Varieties of Religious Experience*, 217.
6 Acts 1:1–2:47; I Corinthians14:5.
7 Hobbes, *Leviathan*, 248–249.
8 Hick, *The Existence of God*, 178–182.
9 Flew and MacIntyre, *New Essays in Philosophical Theology*, 254–260.
10 Plato, *Defence of Socrates, Euthyphro, Crito*, 15–16; Moore, *Principia Ethica*, 61–62, 67–72.
11 Hudson, *The Is/Ought Question*, 177.
12 Kierkegaard, *Fear and Trembling*, 18, 58–59, 86, 24–25.
13 Genesis 1:1, 26–7; Exodus 20:1–17, 20.
14 Temple, *Readings in St John's Gospel*, 48; John 3:18; Hick, *Philosophy of Religion*, 74.
15 I John 4:11; Mark 12:11–12, 28–31; Luke 10:29–37; Caird, *Saint Luke*, 148.
16 Matthew 5:21–6, 38–42, 7:12.
17 Tolstoy, *My Religion*, 35.
18 Jeremias, *the sermon on the mount*, 32–34; Bonhoeffer, *The Cost of Discipleship*, 37; Niebuhr, *An Interpretation of Christian Ethics*, 67, 99.
19 Fletcher, *Situation Ethics*, 26.
20 Butler, *Five Sermons*, 69, 74.
21 Newman, *A Grammar of Assent*, 304; Hick, *The Existence of God*, 185.
22 Kant, *Critique of Practical Reason*, 158, 166; *Religion*, 166.
23 Hick, *The Existence of God*, 191; Mill, *Utilitarianism*, 7; Kant, *Groundwork*, 38.
24 Warnock, *The Object of Morality*, 141; Masham, *Occasional Thoughts in Reference to a Vertuous or Christian Life*, 5.
25 Jessop, *The Christian Morality*, 62–64; I Corinthians 13:1–13.

# 5

# THE SOUL AND THE AFTERLIFE

The soul and the afterlife are two such intertwined ideas that it seems if you believe in a soul, you must believe in an afterlife. But, in fact, that's not the case. You can believe human beings have a soul while also believing that your soul dies when your body dies. Also, you can believe in the afterlife but deny such a thing as a soul.

Clearly, then, we need some clarity on what is meant by the soul and what it is meant by the afterlife, and the different ways in which these beliefs have been associated with each other.

In order to seek such clarity, we shall delve deeper into the differences between, and varieties within, two key positions on the soul and the afterlife: materialism and substance dualism. The first of which is Aristotelian, taking its inspiration from Aristotle, and the second of which is Platonic or Cartesian, taking its inspiration from Plato and Descartes. In each case, we shall find that debates about the existence or nonexistence of the soul, and the possibility or impossibility of life after death, are always also debates about what makes you *you*. Are you *you* because of your mind, and not your body, or are *you* inseparable from your body? As we shall discuss below, this is not a very easy question to answer.

## REDUCTIVIST MATERIALISM

A materialist is someone who thinks that everything that exists either is, or is caused by, physical, material things. Materialism is something usually associated with atheism because a strict materialist won't believe in God, if by God is meant an immaterial and non-physical being.

DOI: 10.4324/9781003568414-6

Consequently, materialism often leads to denial of life after physical death and what is called reductivism about the soul.

For a reductivist, it is unnecessary to believe in an immaterial and non-physical soul when things we usually associate with a soul (our mind, reason, ideas, personality and so on) can be reduced to and explained by something material and physical – our brains – which explains why, if our brain is injured or changes, our mind and personality can change with it.

Within materialist reductivism, as there is no immaterial soul, just our physical brain matter, then there is no life after death, because when our physical brain dies, we die. If all that exists, including our minds and personalities, is, or is dependent upon, physical matter, then there can be no soul and no life after death, because there is no other life or entity before, after, behind and beyond our current physical life and reality.

## ARISTOTELIAN MATERIALISM

Reductivism is a version of materialism that seeks to eliminate soul-talk. There is no soul, only physical brains, and so there is no life after physical death. The only life there is, and the only life you have, is this current physical one.

By contrast, Aristotelian materialism agrees that there is no personal afterlife, but says that there is a soul. This is possible because, in Aristotle, the soul is not principally *noetic* (from the Greek word *nous* for mind) but *hylomorphic* (from the Greek words *hyle* for matter and *morphē* for form). So, in Aristotle, the term soul does not refer to our particular reason, mind, identity, personality, but the fact that we are a particular form of animated matter.

The line most famously associated with Aristotle's view of the soul is that 'the soul is the form of the body'.[1] Let's say there's human-kind, animal-kind and plant-kind. Each of these kinds is made up of physical material or matter (flesh, skin, fibre, fat, blood, sap, sinews, bone), but why does some of this stuff appear and behave in an animal or plant way, and why is other of this stuff *formed* into that which acts and appears in a human way? Because the stuff (matter/body) has been organized into what it is by a different *form* or soul in each case.

So, although Aristotelian materialism employs the language of the soul, it is important to realize that the soul, in Aristotle, is neither uniquely *you* nor uniquely human, and that it does not survive death.

In Aristotle, every organic and living physical thing has a soul, not just humans. Plants and animals, anything which has its own principle of animation, and so which moves itself in some way, has a soul. So, although every human being has a human soul, our human soul does not signify our own unique individual identity as an *I*, but rather our shared identity as humankind, as opposed to plant or animal-kind.

Consequently, the Aristotelian soul cannot survive death, precisely because death is the death of the soul, the end of the life-giving principle that *animated* your form of bodily life. This, for Aristotle, is why all dead bodies (human, animal and plant) decay and dissolve: they have lost their soul and so are losing their *form*. Human corpses decay because the soul that organized this particular bodily matter into its human form has gone, and so just as the physical matter ceases to have its particular form with the loss of its soul, so the individual human being ceases to exist with the death of their body.

## CHRISTIAN MATERIALISM

Aristotle's insight is that we are our bodies, but at the same time are not only our bodies; an insight which leads to what is known as the constitutive view of the human person.

In Aristotelian terms, a constitutive view of the person is the view that a person is constituted by the fact that they have a soul+a body. You cannot be you as a person unless you are a soul+a body, and what makes you *you* is a particular combination of a soul+a body.

In Lynne Rudder Baker, the constitutive view of the person is an opportunity to develop Christian materialism which, on the one hand, agrees with reductivist materialism against Aristotelian materialism that we should eliminate soul-talk altogether, but, on the other hand, argues against both reductivist and Aristotelian materialism that there is an afterlife.

Christian materialism is materialism in the sense that it maintains that human beings, as we exist within this life, are, like every other animal, material beings, and so we exist within, and are dependent upon, our particular physical bodies.

So, for a Christian materialist, there is no soul, if we mean by a soul some part of ourselves which is infinite and non-physical, and which can survive the death of our finite and physical body. Human beings are essentially embodied. Our current body is mortal and finite. And so all human beings die with our current body.

However, although Christian materialism admits that a human person is essentially embodied, like all other animals, it also emphasizes a difference between human beings and other animals, a difference which is itself physical: the complexity of our brain matter when compared to other animals. It's thanks to this difference in physical biology between humans and animals that we are 'ontologically higher': being human is entirely different to being animal because our complex brains enable us to develop what Baker calls 'a first-person perspective'.[2] Unlike other animals, humans have the capacity not just to reflect but to self-reflect and, in doing so, to ask ourselves questions about meaning and purpose, goals and values, who we are and what we should do, as part of a self-conscious sense of our own distinct individual identity.

According to Baker's constitutive view of a person, therefore, a human person is constituted by two things: a body+a first-person perspective. On the one hand, a first-person perspective is unlike the Aristotelian soul, because it is uniquely human (when in Aristotle all organic life has a soul) and uniquely *us*, our own individual self-consciousness (when in Aristotle the human soul is the generic principle of animation or form of life shared by all human beings). On the other hand, a first-person perspective is like the Aristotelian soul because it dies with its body. Our first-person perspective is not produced by an immortal and immaterial soul, but our mortal and material brains, and so it dies when our body dies.

What then is the Christian part of Christian materialism? As Baker points out, the belief that a person is a body+a first-person perspective, such that we die when our body dies, does not preclude an all-powerful God from miraculously recreating our deceased first-person perspective and giving it a new body. Indeed, this is how Baker reads key biblical passages on bodily resurrection: in 1 Corinthians 15, when Paul says that, in the afterlife, we will receive a body, he says it will be a 'changed' and 'glorious' body.

Accordingly, Baker summarizes her view as 'same person, different body, no soul'.[3] Human beings are persons, not because we have a soul, but because we have our own unique first-person perspective+a body. Our first-person perspective developed from and within our physical body in this world, and so when this body dies, our first-person perspective dies with it. Now, to live again as the persons we were, God must recreate our first-person perspective and give it a body. Our first-person perspective needs to be reembodied because there is no such thing as a human person without a body: as human persons are constituted by a first-person perspective+a body, in order to be human and a person in any afterlife, we must again be a first-person perspective+a body. However, although our first-person perspective needs a body in the afterlife, that doesn't mean it needs the same physical body we had in this life. We cannot, and do not need to be, embodied in the same physical body we had in this physical existence to continue to be an individual human person in any future existence. We just need God to give our first-person perspective a new spiritual body for our new spiritual afterlife with him.

## THE PROBLEM OF THESEUS' SHIP

Baker's Christian materialism is a version of recreationism. As human beings are physical beings, when our body dies, we die, and so, to live again, God must recreate what has died.

Sometimes this view is called Christian mortalism. For a Christian mortalist, when you die, you die, body and soul, so everyone who has ever lived is dead right now. Often, when we think of the afterlife, we think of it as something immediate. When your body dies, your soul continues to live and goes to heaven. In Christian moralism, this is not the case. The afterlife is not immediate upon death. Instead, everyone who has ever died is still waiting for the afterlife, which will only happen at the end of time, at the last judgement, when God raises everyone from the dead in bodily resurrection.

Now, a leading criticism of any version of recreationism, including Baker's, is that if you die, such that God has to recreate you or any part of you, then what exists in the afterlife is no longer *you* but a copy.

This criticism is known as the Theseus' ship problem, as first recounted by the 1st/2nd-century Greek philosopher, Plutarch. In the myth of Theseus, he returns to Athens from Crete, where he fought the Minotaur, but as the ship sails back, its wooden boards are constantly rotting away and being replaced by new planks. So, the question is: is Theseus' ship the *same* ship when it gets back from Crete, if all the original boards have slowly been replaced by new ones?

The same question applies to any recreationist view of the afterlife: are you the same person in the afterlife if everything or something essential about you has been remade? We seem to expect some continuity between who we are in this life and who we are in the next. So, to continue to be ourselves in the next life, shouldn't we somehow continue to exist in the next life rather than have to be copied and remade?

## SURVIVING THESEUS' SHIP

Baker's constitutive view tries to get around the problem of Theseus' ship by arguing that, in the afterlife, all that God has to recreate is our first-person perspective. When God gives this recreated first-person perspective a new spiritual body in the afterlife that body becomes ours, and we become ourselves again embodied in it: 'same person, different body'.

Part of Baker's point here again goes back to the Aristotelian soul. Aristotle's soul is a bit like a mould or cookie cutter: whatever material you put into a mould or cookie cutter, it will try to *form* it into a particular shape, just as a human soul in Aristotle forms or moulds physical matter into human shape.

How is it the case that if we have a different body in the afterlife, we are still the same person?

Well, again, think back to Aristotle's language of the soul as the form of the body. Here, a soul needs a body and a body needs a soul, because the soul is that which animates, and so gives form to, a body, by making physical stuff appear, move, act and live in particular ways.

Baker abandons Aristotle's language of the soul for that of first-person perspective, but her point is much the same, following an Aristotelian constitutive view of the person: 'same person, different body, no soul'.

According to Baker, for you to be *you* in the afterlife you need a body+a first-person perspective, because this is what constitutes a person. However, in order for you to have a body in the afterlife, and for it to be your body, God doesn't have to recreate or resurrect the actual deceased body you had in this life. Instead, God only needs to recreate your first-person perspective and attach it to some new spiritual bodily stuff, because your first-person perspective acts like the mould or cookie cutter upon that new bodily stuff and, in effect, makes it into you.

## *THE PRESTIGE* PROBLEM

Whether or not Baker's suggestion that God can remake our first-person perspective and give it a new heavenly body satisfies the problem of Theseus' ship, it raises a related difficulty attending all recreationist views: if, in the afterlife, I am a recreation of what I was, not only am I copy, but it seems there are no absolutely clear limits on how many copies of me can be made, and each of these limitless copies can make a legitimate claim to be me. Let's call this *The Prestige* problem.

In the film *The Prestige* (2006), it turns out that one magician, every time he performs a particular magic trick, makes a clone of himself, and kills that clone, in order to make the trick work. However, it's not clear to the viewer, and maybe to the magician themselves, which is being killed each time: is it the original magician or the clone? Does the magician kill off a clone of himself each time he performs the trick, or did the original magician die the first time the trick was performed, so that now each time the trick is performed, yet another clone of the original magician is made while simultaneously yet another one dies?

Now, what if God, like the magician in *The Prestige*, decided in the afterlife not just to make one copy of me, but lots of them? And what if, unlike the magician, he let all these copies live in the afterlife? Which one of these is *me*? If the original me definitely lives on in some way it is possible to say, 'Here is the original me that still exists, and here are the copies'. But if the original me dies, and then all these copies are made, wouldn't we say either all of these copies are me or none of them are? To use Baker's language, what if God recreated my first-person perspective multiple times, and attached it to lots of new bodies in the afterlife, wouldn't they all equally be me? Indeed, if I die and cease to exist, and God recreates me in the afterlife by remaking my first-person perspective and attaching it to a new body, then which first-person perspective does he choose? Is it the first-person perspective I had when I died, or the one I had as a toddler, or as an adolescent, or during my first job? Couldn't God recreate first-person perspectives I had from various stages throughout my whole life, and then attach them to lots of different new bodies, and, if he did so, wouldn't all of these first-person perspectives+bodies be me?

## PLATONIC SUBSTANCE DUALISM

One apparent way around both the Theseus' ship and *The Prestige* problems is to say that there is some part of you that never dies, and it is this part of you that makes you *you*. That way, there is definite continuity between you now and you in the afterlife because *you* never died. God doesn't recreate you in the afterlife; in fact, death is a gateway into the afterlife for this essential aspect of you.

Arguing in this way leads us away from Aristotelian materialism about the soul into Platonic substance dualism about the soul.

Although Aristotle was Plato's student, what we now call an Aristotelian conception of the soul is different from a Platonic one.

From an Aristotelian viewpoint, the soul is inseparable from the body because it is the body's form, life and animating principle.

From a Platonic viewpoint, the soul is separable from the body, because the soul is principally noetic; it is the individual's mind, ideas and thinking.

So, while for an Aristotelian, the soul is the form of the body, for a Platonist, the soul is something *other* than the body. It is a different *substance* from the body, because it is a mind which has different *properties* from the body. The body is something physical, material, mortal and unthinking; the soul is something non-physical, immaterial, immortal and thinking.

In line with such different views of the soul, an Aristotelian and Platonic conception of the human person is also different.

From an Aristotelian perspective, a human person is a substance constituted by *a soul+a body*: there is no human person who does not exist without a living physical body.

From a Platonic perspective, a human being is comprised of two substances, a *soul(+a body)*, and it is really this first substance, the soul, that constitutes their personhood. As such, a human person can exist without a living physical body.

So, within Aristotelian materialism, human beings are a certain form of matter or physical material, so that an individual human person dies when their body dies.

Within Platonic substance dualism, human beings are two substances – mind and matter – and one substance (mind) can survive the death of the other substance (matter).

## CARTESIAN SUBSTANCE DUALISM

Although a substance dualist view of the soul and the human person is often called Platonic, it's also called Cartesian, given the influence René Descartes upon this position

When Descartes declared *cogito, ergo sum* – I think, therefore I am – he was answering a question he had posed to himself: 'what am I . . .?'[4]

Descartes admits that some obvious answers to this question are bodily, in the sense that they refer to material facts about us in our particular physical and embodied state.

For example, 'what am I?' Well, I am a certain height and weight, I have these particular and distinctive facial features, I dress like this, I live at this particular time, and in this particular place, and so on.

For Descartes, there are at least two problems with these sorts of physical and bodily answers.

First, they don't account for another thing that we all do as human beings, which is non-physical and immaterial: *think*. To Descartes, our thinking mind seems to be very different from our physical body. I can locate, see and touch parts of my body, but I can't locate, see and touch my thinking mind. I might hold opinions, but I can't hold them in the same way I hold a physical object. So, my mind is a different substance from my body.

Second, this other thing that we all do as human beings – *think* – seems to better explain what makes me *me* and you *you*. Each of us has our own physical body, which looks and feels a certain way. But this *I*, this thinking mind and sense of self, goes on behind and beyond all physical characteristics and alterations. Imagine everything physical about you, and everything you experience through your physical body, dissolves away, changes, turns out to be a dream. . . . Is there nothing left over that is *you*?

For Descartes, if you take away or alter everything and anything about your physical, bodily, material substance, there is always something left over which is the non-physical, non-bodily, immaterial substance that is *you*: your thinking mind, and so this is the answer to his question, 'what am I'?

> I am therefore precisely nothing but a thinking thing; that is, a mind, or intellect, or understanding, or reason – words of whose meanings I was previously ignorant. Yet I am a true thing and am truly existing; but what kind of thing? I have said it already: a thinking thing.[5]

## THESEUS'S SHIP AND *THE PRESTIGE* PROBLEMS SOLVED?

In Descartes the question, 'why think there is a soul?' is self-answering: if you didn't have a *soul*, you couldn't *think* at all!

Descartes' *I think, therefore I am* also means *I am, because I think*, so it is your soul, your *thinking* mind, that is *you*. The human soul is every human beings' capacity to be a distinct individual, to be, and to be conscious of themselves, as a thinking *I am*.

Our soul is the unique and distinctive ways in which each of us *think*, by which Descartes means all the different ways in which each of us as individual *I ams* reflect, want, desire, theorize, hate, love, fear, imagine and so on.

As a result, Cartesian substance dualism gives us an argument for the afterlife, which seems to avoid the ship of Theseus and *The Prestige* problems discussed above.

In each of those problems, we needed some essential part of ourselves, the part that made us *us*, to survive death: otherwise it wasn't clear whether what exists in an afterlife is *me*, rather than a copy of me, or whether or not there could legitimately be lots of different copies of me in the afterlife.

In substance dualism, human beings are comprised of two things: mental substance and physical substance, mind or soul and body. It is in the nature of the body to die, as something physical and material, but it is in the nature of the mind or soul to live forever, as something non-physical and immaterial. Our mind-part is our *I am* part, and this survives the death of our body-part. So, it seems there is no Theseus's ship or *Prestige* problem: our soul or *I am* is naturally immortal and survives physical death, so clearly it is *me* in the afterlife and not a copy, and we would definitely know which versions are copies if any were made.

## THE PROBLEM OF THESES' RAFT

However, you may have noticed it's not quite so simple as problems solved. For example, if substance dualism is the belief in disembodied souls in the afterlife it runs into a different version of Theseus' ship problem; let's call this the problem of Theseus' raft.

What if all the boards of Theseus' ship survive the journey from Crete, but everything else rots away? The mast, the sails, the hull, everything has disappeared except for the wooden boards that made the deck. Wouldn't we say that Theseus' ship has ceased to exist and, although some piece of that ship still survives, what remains is no longer the ship, but something else, just a raft?

Similarly, with ourselves. If our soul or thinking mind survives into the afterlife, but without our body, aren't we now someone or something else from who or what we were in this life?

Admittedly, the substance dualist might just respond by saying the difference between the raft and the ship is only apparent: what has survived is not a raft but, in fact, the essential part of the ship. However, the Christian materialist may still wonder whether, in ceasing to be embodied, we have still lost something that was essential to the person that we were in this life, so that even if some supposedly essential part of us survives, we are no longer who we were before, and so more like Theseus' raft than his ship?

One way around the problem of Theseus' raft is for the substance dualist to maintain that immortal souls are, in fact, reembodied in the afterlife and that they are reembodied into the *same* body that they had in this life. In other words, a substance dualist might believe in bodily resurrection, and they might believe in either immediate or future bodily resurrection. That is, they might believe that God reembodies the immortal soul immediately after death or at some future time.

Now, there are a few issues with believing that the immortal soul receives the same body it had in this life. For one, that body is here on earth rotting and decaying. So, clearly the immortal soul cannot receive either immediately or in the future *that* body. In which case, it seems as though the substance dualist who believes in bodily resurrection is back amongst some version of the problem of Theseus' ship. At least one part of us in the afterlife is a copy of what we were in this life. And this leads to further questions: if God is able to recreate my body and place my immortal soul back within it, which version of my body does he recreate? Will it be a recreation of my youthful body, or my middle-aged body, or the body I had when I died? Will it be recreated with any injuries or disabilities?

## THE BUTTERFLY ANALOGY

One response to these questions available to a substance dualist employs the butterfly analogy, which helps to explain why, although you have a body in the afterlife, and it is your body, it is a new spiritual version of your body.

A caterpillar turns into a butterfly. A caterpillar body is not the same as a butterfly body, but a caterpillar body becomes a butterfly body, and it is the same individual creature that is caterpillar-embodied and butterfly-embodied: the caterpillar did not die, and then there was a butterfly, the butterfly emerges from and is in continuity with the caterpillar.

Similarly, when the soul is embodied in the afterlife, the nature and experience of its embodiment in the afterlife must be different from the nature and experience of its embodiment in this life, as the caterpillar body is different from the butterfly body. But that doesn't mean that our new body in the afterlife does not emerge from the previous body, or from the immortal soul itself, just as the butterfly body emerges from the caterpillar body.

A bodily afterlife for the immortal soul would have to be a life in a new non-physical and spiritual body, because it is a non-physical and spiritual life after this physical one. This means that any body we have in the afterlife cannot be a body as we currently understand it.

Body in this life means comprised of physical or material substance, but body in the afterlife must mean some non-physical or immaterial substance. So, perhaps the body we have in the afterlife more closely resembles or is connected with our immaterial soul itself, such that the body we have in the afterlife is still our body but in its non-physical butterfly rather than physical caterpillar state. As the 18th-century substance dualist, Samuel Clarke, put it: 'The plain meaning of St Paul is only this, that the Body which in this present state is dissolvable and corruptible, shall after the Resurrection, by the Power of God, be made incorruptible'.[6]

## HARD PROBLEM OF CONSCIOUSNESS

As well as raising questions about whether, and if so, in what sense, we have bodies in the afterlife, substance dualism also faces the criticism that it is undermined by our current bodiliness itself.

Cartesian or Platonic (what we might call 'classical') substance dualism maintains that mind cannot come from matter, because what is thinking (mind) cannot come from what is unthinking (matter). As a result, classical substance dualism maintains that there are two substances that make up human beings: mental substance and physical substance. As thinking cannot come from the physical substance of our bodies, it must come from the mental substance of our souls.

In response, the materialist is not dualist (two) but monist (one): human beings are not made up of two substances (mind and matter), but one substance (matter), which accounts for everything, including mind. Thinking *does* come from physical matter, not least brain matter, so there is no such thing as non-physical mental substance or the soul. What the substance dualist mistakenly calls an immaterial soul can actually be described in material or physical terms: I am me, and I have this particular mind and way of thinking, not because I have an immaterial soul, but because of the unique material way in which the electrical currents of my neurons physically fire.

One response to a materialist who denies the soul by reducing mind to the physical brain is to press what is known as the hard problem of consciousness.

Here, the problem is that although biology and neuroscience may help to explain the physical act of thinking, that doesn't seem to account for how we personally direct our thoughts as part of a self-conscious mind. So, a substance dualist may, in fact, agree with the materialist that thinking can be explained by the physical processes of the brain but still reject the notion that our mind can be reduced just to physical processes.

Descartes, for example, recognizes that animals have brains and that they function with what we might call thoughts. *Do this, get that, that hurts, eat now, run from here*. However, even if these are thoughts resulting from having a physical brain, they do not add up to a mind. For Descartes, animals are robots, without souls or minds, programmed by God to react automatically to certain kinds of thoughts or brain processes.

So, from a Cartesian perspective, there is a sense in which the human body, including our brain, is, like an animal's, robotic. Our brain is a machine for thinking, which may well be programmed with certain kinds of thoughts to direct, and to react to, the wider body. *Do this, get that, that hurts, eat now, run from here*. But even if thinking is a physical action of our brain matter that still leaves open the hard problem of consciousness.

If the physical organ of the brain thinks, in the same way that the physical organ of the eye sees or the skin touches, what's this *I* that is aware of itself thinking, seeing, touching? Why don't we just have robotic thoughts, *get up, get dressed, eat this, go over there*, rather than self-aware thoughts, *I don't want to get up, I can't wear that, I find this delicious, I'll go over there if we go somewhere else tomorrow*. More than this, why is it that I seem to have a sense not only of my own subjective self and inner life but also of the fact that *you* must have one of your own as another self-conscious *I*? Where does the concept of *you* let alone *me* come from?

These questions, as part of the hard problem of consciousness, confirm for the classical substance dualist that, although we have a physical brain that can think, we still need an immortal soul to account for how that physical brain is directed to think as an individual mind.

## EMERGENT DUALISM

As well as the hard problem of consciousness, another available response to a materialist reduction of mind to matter is to be an emergent, rather than classical, substance dualist.

The classical substance dualist believes, in effect, that our immortal souls pre-date our mortal bodies. Our soul doesn't come out of our bodies because a physical and unthinking substance cannot produce a non-physical and thinking substance. Instead, our souls are, in some sense, housed, encased or sit within our body. In Plato's *Symposium*, Socrates recounts a creation myth where God judges in which bodies to place immortal souls, based on which bodies seem to be most suitable to the personality of the souls. Similarly, Descartes describes the body as a statute crafted purposefully around each soul.

Unlike the classical substance dualist, the emergent substance dualist doesn't believe our souls pre-date our bodies but, instead, that our souls emerge from our bodies. In this sense, emergent dualism, unlike classical dualism, partly agrees with materialism.

An emergent dualist agrees with the materialist that our mind, identity, personality, consciousness and first-person perspective come from our particular material brain. The difference, for the emergent dualist, is that once our thinking mind emerges from the physical processes of our brain, it no longer depends upon them. Once the mind emerges from matter, it becomes an entirely different substance from that which is material and mortal: it becomes our immaterial and immortal soul.

The American philosopher, William Hasker, is the key proponent of emergent dualism, and he employs the analogy of an electromagnet to illustrate his position.[7] An electromagnet is a visible physical machine, but when you turn it on it produces an invisible magnetic field, which has properties and behaviours different from the machine from which it emerges. More than this, even when you turn off a certain kind of electromagnet, it leaves behind the magnetic field it created.

Like the electromagnet, with the human person, each of us would not have our immaterial mind if there were not first our material body. And, just as the type of magnetic field generated depends on the type of physical magnet switched on, so the specific workings and experiences of our material bodies help to influence our immaterial minds. But, once mind emerges from the body, it is something *other* than the body, which can survive its death, in the same way the electromagnetic field is not the same as the physical electromagnet and survives even after it is turned off.

## THE MIND/BODY PROBLEM

Arguing that the mind or soul is a different substance from the body, but that it emerges from the body, means that emergent dualism has at least one advantage over classical dualism: it helps to mitigate against what is called the mind/body problem, which is the question of how mind and body interact if they are two different substances.

The mind/body problem is most famously associated with Descartes, thanks to what the philosopher Gilbert Ryle termed 'the ghost in the machine'.

In Cartesian substance dualism, it seems like the mind is an immaterial ghost caught within a material machine. A ghost is able to interact directly with other immaterial entities in its spiritual realm, but, in haunting a house, a ghost cannot touch things in the physical realm, like the walls it passes through. Similarly, in Descartes, mind and body are defined in oppositional terms. Physical substance is what Descartes calls 'extended' and mental substance 'unextended'. In other words, it is only material bodies, and not immaterial souls, that exist *out there* in space and time. No matter how hard I think, 'move that stone', it will not move, and no matter how hard you throw a stone, it cannot hit a thought or idea. But if mental and physical substances are so different from each other that they cannot interact, doesn't this mean there is a gap between your mind and body? And, if there is a gap between mind/body, because mind and body operate within different realms or spheres of influence, like ghosts in houses or oil on water, how does our mind move our body?

In answer to such questions, Descartes asks whether a little part of our physical brain (the pineal gland) might act as a point of contact between body and soul, allowing the immaterial mind to engage with the physical body. Descartes' suggestion is not always clear and still makes the soul seem like a separate entity or ghost, which sits behind the machine of the brain using the pineal gland as a lever to bridge the gap between two otherwise independent substances or realms.

A follower of Descartes, Gottfried Leibniz, went even further with the absolute separation between mind/body. According to Leibniz's 'pre-established harmony', your body is like a robot or machine that God has pre-programmed to line up with what God foresaw your thoughts to be throughout your life. Mind cannot directly influence body because they are two separate substances, so, if you think now, 'I'll stick out my tongue' it may feel like the thought and decision to stick out your tongue is causing your tongue to stick out, but that's not the case. Instead, God just foresaw at creation that you would will, in this moment, to stick out your tongue, and so pre-programmed your body to harmonize with your mind.

## MANICHAEISM AND THE HOLY GHOST IN THE MACHINE PROBLEM

Substance dualism doesn't just come up against 'the ghost in the machine' problem but also what I'll call 'the holy ghost in the machine problem', a problem most notably associated with Manichaeism.

The Manicheans were followers of the 3rd-century Persian philosopher, Mani, and they had a controversial relationship with early Christian philosophical theology, not least because Augustine initially followed, before finally rejecting, Manichaeism.

The Manicheans were substance dualists, who argued that, as there are two separate substances that comprise reality, there must be two gods who govern over each of them: the good god of the mind or soul, who governs over the spiritual realm, and the devil or evil god of body or matter who governs over the physical realm.

Such radical dualism provides an answer to some fundamental questions raised by classical substance dualism. For example, if the soul or mind doesn't come from the body, how and why did it get into the body? And, why is it that the soul or mind is really us, such that the death of the mortal and material body is freedom and release for the immortal and immaterial soul from that which holds it captive? The answer for the Manicheans is that the good god of perfect mind and eternal life created human souls, and the evil god of decaying and limited matter created human bodies to capture the divine spirits or souls of the good god. In consequence, the Manicheans, in line with a later Christian variant, the Cathars or Albigensians, taught against sex and marriage, because having children only perpetuated the capture of the divine spirit in demonic flesh.

Classical substance dualism rejects the Manichean positing of two rival gods as well as two opposing substances. However, even

Descartes wonders whether this physical bodily realm may be ruled over by a deceiving demon, just as Plato describes this physical realm as a shadowy imperfect reflection of perfect immaterial Forms or Ideas. Both Platonic and Cartesian substance dualism are forms of what's called idealism: philosophical and theological systems that prize mind over matter, ideas over bodies, and so associate the mind or the soul with that which is pure, ideal, divine in contrast to the body or matter which is associated with that which is corrupted, limited, fallen.

Consequently, Manichaeism may be regarded as a radical, but logical, conclusion of substance dualism. The soul or mind is not just a ghost within a machine, a mind separate from the body it exists within, but a holy ghost within an infernal machine, where the mind or soul, through death and the afterlife, seeks liberation from an alien, if not evil, body that ensnares it in this life.

## FREEWILL AND NECESSITY

Hasker's emergent dualism aims to avoid classical dualism's tendency towards 'ghost in the machine' and 'holy ghost in the infernal machine' problems.

If the soul emerges from the body, then the mind is not trapped within the body in any negative sense, because the physical processes of our body are not separate from or antithetical to our mind but essential to its generation. Indeed, it is because emergent dualism recognizes mind as a substance that emerges from the body that it allows for ways in which mind is a substance that influences the body from which it emerges. As Hasker points out, mind, consciousness, and the soul do not simply emerge from the physical activity of our brains. Instead, once our mind has emerged, it is a substance which has physical effects upon our body, determining our thought patterns and behaviours. The type of mind I have actively influences my thinking, feelings, even aspects of my physical appearance, and so on.

It is in this way that emergent dualism stresses what is called libertarian freewill, as part of emphasising the role our minds or souls have in freely shaping who we are and what we do. Libertarian freewill in emergent substance dualism stands in contrast to the tendency towards determinism within Cartesian substance dualism, not least in Leibniz's pre-established harmony, as mentioned above.

In Leibniz, God has foreseen what we will think and determined our bodies to line up with our thoughts. For this to work that must mean my thoughts are not free or random but follow a necessary path known in advance by God. Leibniz's view is something like this:

> When I have thoughts to do or choose something, and my body responds, it's not those thoughts that make my body move. My body moves because God has programmed my body to line up with my thoughts. So, my body is not free, but determined by God.
>
> But this also means, I can't change the thoughts I have, the choices and desires I want to make and fulfil, the things I want my body to do. My thoughts, wants, desires follow necessary patterns as foreseen by God. It is because I think and will predictably and necessarily that God can programme my body to line up with my thoughts.

Interestingly, Leibniz doesn't think his view denies human freewill. Instead, he makes a distinction between what he calls 'moral necessity' and 'metaphysical necessity'.[8]

Metaphysical necessity is something like 2+2=4 or any other laws of physics and mathematics. These are necessary laws that must be true or obtain in all possible worlds. Nothing, not even God, can change 2+2=4, it is a 'metaphysical necessity'.

However, while God had to create a world in which 2+2=4, he didn't have to create a world with *you* in it. You are, and act from, a moral, rather than metaphysical, necessity. When God creates the world, he plans for it to be, as Leibniz famously put it, 'the best of all possible worlds', and every person God creates helps the world to be the best that it can be. Given evil people in the world, it may be hard for us to see how everyone's actions contribute to what's best, but, for Leibniz, all actions, somehow, help to fulfil God's plan for the best possible world.

Let's take the example of 'doubting Thomas' in the New Testament. When God created Thomas the disciple, he knew that he would doubt Christ's resurrection. God also made it so that the movements of Thomas' body would harmonize with his decision to doubt, so that as Thomas seeks to be convinced that Christ has returned from the dead, his hands reach out and touch Jesus' wounds. God foresaw Thomas' scepticism, and pre-programmed his bodily movements to coincide with his thoughts, and God did all this because he foresaw that Thomas' doubt would, in some way, contribute to the best of all possible worlds. And, this is the same for every person that God creates: every person that exists only does so because God foresaw how we would help to bring about the best of all possible worlds.

Leibniz admits, then, that human beings think and will by necessity. Thomas could not have chosen to think and act differently. But his point is that this isn't a lack of freedom or choice, like the metaphysical necessity of 2+2=4, because each of us always thinks and wills as the person we truly are. In this sense, we do not act by an external metaphysical necessity universal to all possible worlds, but according to a unique moral necessity internal to us. God made us because he knew the sort of persons we would be, how we would think and will, and the sort of actions we would want our bodies to perform, and that's why he made us, and made it so that our physical bodies line up with our mental thoughts. To say that we are not free because God foreknows exactly how we will think and will as true to ourselves is a bit like saying a flower isn't free because it cannot choose whether or not to blossom: a flower has to blossom to be true to itself, Thomas has to doubt Christ to be Thomas. Freedom for Leibniz isn't arbitrary and random choice, it is the moral necessity of each of us always being who we are and who God knows us to be.

## OPEN THEISM

Leibniz's necessity follows his Cartesian substance dualism. As he strongly divides mental and physical substance, he has to explain how our bodily movements coincide with our mental movements or thoughts: God foresees what our mind will necessarily think and choose, and predetermines our body to harmonize with our mind.

In moving away from Cartesian substance dualism, Hasker's emergent dualism is able to emphasize libertarian freewill over Leibnizian necessity.

In emergent dualism, like Cartesian dualism, the mind is a different substance from body. However, in emergent dualism, unlike Cartesian dualism, our mind emerges from our body, so there is a close connection between our mind and our body and how, together, they form us as an individual person. Here, once the mind emerges as a different substance from the body, it is free, and it is free thinking that helps to determine what my body does, and who I become, not any pre-determined necessity.

So, for the emergent dualist and libertarian about freewill, Leibniz's attempted distinction between moral and metaphysical necessity fails. If my mind or soul cannot control my body directly, and if my mind or soul cannot think or will contrary to how God knows, in advance, I will think or act, then both my body and my mind are not free, and I am not a person but a machine, pre-determined to function in necessary and unavoidable ways.

As a result, emergent dualism is consistent with, not just libertarian freewill, but what is called 'open theism'. An open theist, like Hasker, maintains that the future is open and unknown, not just to human beings, but to God as well.

To return again to the example of Thomas, for the open theist, it must be the case that Thomas *chooses* to doubt Christ and that he might have *chosen* to act differently, and, in doing so, influenced both his own character and wider events in any number of different and possible ways. Even though God will respond to the things I choose to do, he doesn't foreknow in advance all that I will think and do, because that is up to me, and what I think and do helps to shape who I am as well as what the future will be.

From a Leibnizian perspective, an emphasis upon libertarian freewill and the future's openness places limits on God's omnipotence and omniscience by limiting his foreknowledge. God cannot be all-knowing if he doesn't know what the future is, and he cannot be all-powerful if what the future is lies outside his control.

However, from an open theist perspective, neither God's omnipotence nor omniscience is limited if the future is open to human free choice. The fact that God does not, and cannot, know the future doesn't limit his omniscience, because even an all-knowing being can only know what is logically possible, and it is not logically possible for God, or anyone, to know the future, because it doesn't exist yet. Similarly, leaving the future open to free human decision-making doesn't limit God's power. First, again, even an all-powerful being can only control what it is logically possible to control, and the future, as it doesn't exist yet, lies beyond anyone's power to foresee or determine. Second, human freedom doesn't limit God's power if it is God himself who has freely chosen to allow human beings to be free. Even if, theoretically, God could use his power to determine human thought and action, in reality, he hasn't: God himself has chosen to leave the future open to human freewill by making human beings in his image as free agents with self-responsibility both for ourselves and the future world we live in.

## DOUBLE PREDESTINATION

Whether, and if so in what sense, human beings possess freewill has important consequences for the afterlife, not least when it comes to the question of fairness.

A basic belief in the afterlife is not just that we live again after this one, but that our afterlife is some sort of reward or punishment for how we behaved in this life. If our mind and/or body isn't free, are we genuinely responsible for what we've done, and deserving of any reward or punishment we receive?

John Calvin helped to place particular pressure on the question of fairness with his doctrine of double predestination. According to this view, God's foreknowledge is such that he knows in advance who will be saved and who will be damned, meaning that who is saved and who is damned is already predetermined or predestined. None of the actions any of us perform in this life can change whether or not we are going to heaven or hell.

On the one hand, double predestination sounds unfair, because it seems like I could try my hardest in this life to be a member of what Calvin calls 'the elect', and not in fact be one, because God has already predestined who is elected for salvation.

On the other hand, Calvin's position does help to make a bit more sense of Leibniz's moral necessity.

In Leibniz, God creates us foreknowing who we are and what we will necessarily want to do, and so predetermines our bodies to act in line with our thoughts. In Calvin, God's predestination is also a feature of God knowing fundamentally who we are at our creation. God doesn't need to wait to see how we behave in the world to know who is a sinner and who is a saint, because he already foreknows who we are, and so he predetermines who to save because he can already foresee who is deserving of salvation.

In other words, Calvin's double predestination, like Leibniz's necessitarianism, preserves God's omniscience and omnipotence by making it impossible for God to make a mistake. Calvin describes grace as 'irresistible', by which he means if God chooses to save you, that's it, you're saved. What if God tried to save people who didn't deserve it or who could refuse to be saved? That would make grace resistible and undermine God's perfect power and knowledge. God wouldn't be all-knowing, because he wouldn't know in advance who is a saint and who is a sinner, who would say 'Yes' to, and who is deserving of, grace. God wouldn't be all-powerful, because human beings would have the power to say 'Yes' or 'No' to grace, which would give humans power over God: rather than divine freewill predetermining to whom he would offer grace, human freewill would determine to whom he would offer grace.

Just as there are touchpoints between Calvin's double predestination and Leibniz's moral necessity, it is the case that open theists and libertarians about freewill who reject Leibnizian necessitarianism also reject Calvinist predestination.

For the libertarian and open theist, God cannot know who in advance who will be saved and who will be damned, because God cannot know in advance the sort of persons that we will choose to be and the actions that we will choose to perform.

Does libertarian freewill mean that grace is no longer irresistible? For Samuel Clarke, a substance dualist who opposed both Calvin and Leibniz, the answer is an emphatic, 'Yes!' Clarke prefers the libertarian language of human beings 'cooperating' with grace via our own freewill. God does not predetermine to whom he will offer grace as though human life is a matter of fate. Instead, God offers salvation to all human beings in Christ as an act of grace, and it is the responsibility of each of us as individuals to respond to God's salvific grace by freely choosing to make our future lives and actions Christ-like.

## PERSONAL IDENTITY

Clarke's libertarian account of freewill is a reminder that the question of fairness with respect to the afterlife doesn't just concern whether or not you deserve the reward or punishment you receive in the afterlife, but whether it is really *you* in the afterlife being rewarded or punished.

According to Clarke, the only way of ensuring that you are *you* in the afterlife is 'by securing a Principle of *Personal Individuality*', and this is only possible by believing in the 'natural immortality' of the soul.[9] For the rewards and punishments received in the afterlife to be fair and just, you must be *self*-responsible for what you did in this life but also continue to be your*self* in the afterlife. Libertarian freewill makes me self-responsible for what I did in this life, and so deserving of any rewards or punishment I receive in the afterlife. Meanwhile, the immortal soul ensures that I continue to be myself in the afterlife, so that it is the same person who is receiving rewards or punishment in the afterlife for what they did in this life.

However, there is the question of whether the belief in an immortal soul is as secure a 'Principle of Personal Individuality' as Clarke thinks it is?

Like our bodies, our mind, personality, perspective, identity, way of thinking go through a number of changes in our lifetimes. In the afterlife which of these will we have: the one I had when I was a teenager, or when I was middle-aged, or just the one when I died?

If it's the case, as it seems to be for the substantive dualist, that the mind or soul just continues to exist as the body dies, does that mean that the mind or soul that survives death is simply the one the person had when they died? If so, is that fair, if, for various reasons they had not seemed fully themselves for the last years of their life, perhaps because, just before they died, they had Alzheimer's or a brain injury that severely altered their personality?

A substance dualist might try and answer these questions by maintaining that your mental substance, your immortal soul, as it pre-exists or emerges from your body, contains your essential identity in a way which exists beyond and behind any ways in which your limited current body allows you to present yourself physically.

Here, I'll use the analogy of a typewriter:

> Let's say a great playwright only has access to one typewriter, which becomes faulty: the colour of the ink keeps changing

and failing, as does the font size, and some of the letters stop appearing. When you receive the playwright's script in the post it doesn't seem like it's from the great playwright, but it is: he is still there behind that damaged or limited physical typewriter trying to do the typing.

Similarly, physical changes to our brain may limit the ways in which we can and do think, and how we are able to express our thoughts to others, just as the physical typewriter limits the ways in which the great playwright can write. However, these physical changes and limitations don't alter the fact that there is a mind, the same *I am*, sitting behind the physical brain trying to do the thinking, in the same way it is the same great playwright sitting behind the faulty typewriter trying to do the typing.

Now, what the great playwright needs to write fully and freely as themselves is a new typewriter, and what the immortal soul needs is a new body. The hope in the afterlife for the substance dualist is that it is the soul or *I am* behind any physical changes or confines that continues to exist, and is able to fully realize itself in a new spiritual life and body, away from the limitations of this current physical one.

## CONCLUSION: THOMAS AQUINAS AND THE SOUL

Whatever approach is taken to the soul and the afterlife, whether materialist or dualist, it opens up a series of difficult questions about the nature of mind/body, the relationship between mind/body, and if, in the afterlife, we possess the same mind and/or body?

Confronted by such questions, it is impossible to end this topic, as with most topics in philosophical theology, without mentioning Thomas Aquinas, who tried to effect a compromise between the materialist and dualist positions.

On the one hand, Aquinas agrees with Aristotelian materialism that all organic life possesses a soul, and what constitutes you as a person is your rational soul+your body. For Aquinas, it is in the womb that the human embryo develops through, first, the vegetative stage of the soul possessed by all plant life, then the sensitive stage of the soul possessed by all animal life, and, finally, the stage of ensoulment, when God directly infuses the rational soul into the developing human being.

On the other hand, Aquinas agrees with Platonic substance dualism that the human rational soul, infused by God, is immortal, and so survives the death of the physical body.

Thus, Aquinas agrees with a materialist constitutive view of the person, that we are only ourselves as unique individuals when we are our soul+our body, because it is the fact that we are a particular embodied rational soul that makes us a distinctive individual. But, at the same time, Aquinas agrees with the substantive dualist that, as it were, one half of what makes us a person, our mind or rational soul, is immaterial and immortal and so survives the death of our physical body.

Aquinas' compromise relies on, and makes sense in light of, the belief in a future bodily resurrection. Aristotelians are right that we need a body to be individual human persons, so we are only once again ourselves when we receive bodily resurrection at the last judgement. But Platonists are also right that we have an immortal soul, and so some part of us survives death, and is waiting for bodily resurrection right now, so there is definite continuity between this life and the afterlife because your rational soul never dies.

Aquinas' attempted compromise between materialism and dualism runs into a tension of its own. If everyone who dies has an immortal soul which exists in the afterlife as soon as they die, but all these souls are awaiting their resurrected bodies, is it the case that each disembodied soul is not yet fully a person? Is everyone who has died only, in some sense, partly themselves, and only fully again themselves at the time of the last judgement and bodily resurrection? What personal identity do disembodied souls possess if they are the soul of a person, but also not yet fully the person they were when they died?

These questions for Aquinas' attempted compromise highlight how central to debates about the soul and the afterlife is the question of what makes you *you*? And, in fact, changing the nature of that question is another way of finding a point of agreement between Aristotle's materialism and Plato's substance dualism.

In places, Plato argues that the soul is immortal and so survives the death of the body, but is then reincarnated into a different body, and so becomes, effectively, another person.

Similarly, Aristotle suggests that one part of the soul, the abstract activity of thinking he calls 'the agent intellect', does survive death, but without any personal memories or characteristics of the deceased person.

So, another way around many of the questions explored in this chapter is not to deny the existence of the soul and the afterlife, but to question whether it is *personal*. Although it raises its own set of difficult questions, it is possible to believe in the soul and the afterlife, but to say they are not *yours* anyway.

## NOTES

1 Aristotle, *On the Soul*, 412ª1.
2 Baker, 'Material Persons', 157
3 Baker, 'Resurrecting Material Persons', 315.
4 Descartes, *Meditations*, 65.
5 Descartes, *Meditations*, 65.
6 Clarke, 'Letter to Dodwell', 13.
7 Hasker, *Emergent Self*, 190.
8 Leibniz, *Leibniz-Clarke Correspondence*, 56–57.
9 Clarke, *Third Defense*, 88.

6

# EVIL, PROVIDENCE AND MIRACLES

*The* problem of evil and suffering: actually, there are two problems. Because of the nature of our environment and the sort of beings we are, all human beings suffer during their lives. The problem of evil arises for Christians and other theists, who believe that the world is not just a brute fact but was created by God. In the religious context, human beings are both God's creatures and also rational beings, who look at the world and wonder why God made it like this. The problem of evil concerns the apparent contradiction between the presence in the world of natural and moral evil, and the belief that an omnipotent and omni-benevolent God created it. Natural evil refers to the features of the world which cause suffering, such as diseases, hurricanes and floods; moral evil to suffering caused by such human actions as violence, torture and theft. If an infinitely powerful God created the universe from nothing, he is entirely responsible for the way it is, and for the presence in it of both kinds of evil. If God is also all-loving, it is hard to understand why he created such a world and not one that contains no evil and (in consequence) no suffering at all.

Or is it? Theodicy ('justifying God', a term invented by Leibniz) is the Christian response to the problem of evil. It attempts to explain why an infinitely powerful and all-loving God chose to create a world that contains evil and suffering. Traditional Christian theodicy, associated with Augustine of Hippo, refers back to the Genesis myth of the Fall. Although they enjoyed a perfect relationship with God, Adam and Eve, the first man and woman, chose to disobey God. As a result, their perfect relationship with God came to an end, and they are now at a distance from God; sin (breaking

DOI: 10.4324/9781003568414-7

God's laws) and death entered the world; and, according to the doctrine of original sin, human nature was so damaged by the fall that human beings inherit an inclination towards sinning.

But does this myth suggest that what happened was the fault of human beings, who are mere, finite creatures, or of God, who made them and everything else from nothing? Below, we examine the case against God, for creating a world which contains evil and suffering, and for allowing it to continue unchecked, which for some philosophers makes the Christian conception of God untenable, together with theodicies put forward in God's defence. On both sides of the argument, we should look out for the protagonists' views about what they regard as God's purpose in creating the world; the views of theists and non-theists are likely to be different.

## THE CASE AGAINST GOD

### *THE INCONSISTENT TRIAD*

In his *Dialogues Concerning Natural Religion*, David Hume refers to a trilemma or 'inconsistent triad', attributed to the Ancient Greek philosopher, Epicurus, which encapsulates the challenge that theists face when trying to reconcile evil and suffering in the world with its creation by an omnipotent and omnibenevolent God:

> Is he [God] willing to prevent evil, but not able? then is he impotent.
> Is he able, but not willing? then is he malevolent.
> Is he both able and willing? whence then is evil?

For Richard Robinson, this trilemma demonstrates that the God of Christianity cannot exist. The concept is 'self-contradictory', because a world made by an all-powerful and all-benevolent God would contain no pain and suffering. We should note that, for Robinson, God's only possible purpose, in creating a world, would have been to make a place where his creatures would be happy. But that is not the only possible view of God's purpose.

Though we may not agree that suffering in the world makes God's existence a logical impossibility, it is hard not to sympathize with Anthony Flew's frustration at theists' refusal to regard even extremes of suffering as evidence against their beliefs, What does the assertion that God loves his human creatures, as 'a father loves his children', actually mean? Is there any event that theists would accept as sufficient ground for admitting that God does not exist, or does not love human beings? Flew gives the example of a terminally ill child. Their earthly father desperately tries to help, but his heavenly father seems to do nothing. When challenged, the theist qualifies his position and explains that God's love is not like human love and is beyond comprehension. But what would have to happen to force the theist, not just 'morally and wrongly', but 'logically and rightly', to admit that God does not exist, or is not all-loving? The theistic hypothesis is not 'genuinely experimental', because the theist will never allow any evidence to count against it.[1]

## HOW MUCH MISERY IS THERE IN THE WORLD?

We met Cleanthes, Philo and Demea in Chapter 2. They also debate the problem of evil and suffering, in the context of God's existence and nature, and the extent to which they can be known by means of natural reason, without the aid of revelation. Demea rejects the kind of conclusions expressed by Robinson and Flew. Yes, as such examples as 'a hospital full of diseases' or 'a field of battle strewed with carcases' show, human life is full of misery. But evil and suffering have a purpose; they bring home to people 'the truth of religion' and make them turn to God. Philo agrees that there is general human and animal misery, which is increased for human beings by their capacity for reflection. Cleanthes, however, insists that human unhappiness is less common than Demea and Philo believe. Philo then challenges Cleanthes' claim that God's 'moral attributes' resemble those of human beings. Theists believe that God is infinitely powerful and benevolent, so why is there not more human and animal happiness? He repeats Epicurus' trilemma and comments that the only purposes discernible in nature are 'the preservation alone of individuals and the propagation of the species'.

Surprisingly, Cleanthes' response is not that the issue of God's existence and nature cannot be tied to the sum of happiness in the world, because God's purpose, in making it, was not (primarily) the creation of a hedonistic paradise. Instead, and mistakenly, he allows

Philo to set the terms of the debate, accepting that conclusive proof of human unhappiness would be 'the end at once of all religion', thus fatally undermining his position. And he cannot fall back on the sort of defence that Demea proffers, that the misery of this world will be put right in a future life; he dismisses talk of human beings' ultimate destiny as mere speculation. The only way for him to establish God's benevolence is to show that, here and now, more human beings are happy than miserable. Triumphantly, Philo points out the impossibility of calculating the balance of pleasure and pain in the world; Cleanthes' whole position hinges on a claim that cannot be decided either way. And, even if there is more happiness than unhappiness in the world, this does not explain why God allows 'any misery at all'. Human suffering may be compatible with God's infinite power and goodness, but it makes it impossible to prove he has these attributes. As the world presents a 'mixed and confused' picture of happiness and unhappiness, God's attributes cannot be inferred from it.

## PERHAPS GOD IS NOT INFINITE

Cleanthes now concedes the impossibility of proving God's infinite goodness and power from the mixed evidence available in the world. However, if God is only 'finitely perfect', a satisfactory account can be given of natural and moral evil. Philo disagrees, because someone, unacquainted with the world, who was told that it had been produced by a 'very good, wise and powerful', though finite, God would expect something better. Evil and suffering in the world may be compatible with the existence of a finitely good and powerful God, but they rule out the possibility of inferring God's existence or nature solely from what we find in the world. If nothing in a house works properly, it would be in vain for the architect to claim that alterations would make it even worse. We would say that a skilled and well-intentioned architect would have designed a better house in the first place.

## I COULD HAVE DESIGNED A BETTER WORLD MYSELF

Philo identifies factors that intensify suffering. The world operates according to 'general laws', the rigidity of which often causes pain.

Without revealing his existence, God could intervene in the world, to turn potentially damaging events into beneficial ones, and could have given human beings greater powers to surmount the difficulties they face. Philo admits that, if God's goodness could be established on *a priori* grounds, the world's defects might be reconcilable with it, but their presence removes any possibility of inferring the goodness of even a finite God from a world containing so many ills, which suggest only 'blind nature', not an intelligent cause. Philo's now overt scepticism offends Demea, but Cleanthes points out Demea's failure to appreciate the implications of the theological position he shares with so many religiously orthodox people. Stressing the misery of human existence, and the 'incomprehensibility' of God's ways, may have driven people towards religion in pre-scientific times, as their only possible protection against the dangers of a world which they did not understand, but will not work in a more enlightened era.[2]

## HUMAN BEINGS ARE PUNISHED FOR WHAT NATURE DOES EVERY DAY

The utilitarian philosopher, John Stuart Mill, concerned with the maximization of human happiness, agrees with Philo that the order of nature does not suggest its creation by a just and benevolent God. Mill puts it bluntly: the kind of wrongdoing for which human beings are hanged or imprisoned are 'nature's everyday performances'. Murder, the most serious human crime, nature commits against 'every being that lives', often in ways that involve extremes of suffering. Mill condemns the 'sophistry' of philosophical theologians, who argue that the present level of human suffering is necessary, in order to 'prevent greater'. If, as Christians believe, an omnipotent God created everything apart from himself, there is misery in the world because God wills it. Experience of the world makes it impossible to claim that it resembles 'the work of a being at once good and omnipotent', or to argue from the world as we find it to such a God as its creator. Like Philo, Mill looks at the world from a wholly human and utilitarian perspective. He believes that actions are right or wrong to the extent that they promote happiness or cause pain, so he cannot comprehend why God should have created a world that was not the pleasantest possible place for human beings to inhabit. As in his treatment of religion in *Utilitarianism*, he fails to consider the possibility that God's prime purpose in creating the world may not have been human happiness.[3]

John Mackie focuses on moral evil and human freewill. To understand why a wholly good God gave men freewill, it must be assumed that it is better that human beings should act freely and sometimes do wrong than that they should be 'innocent automata', acting rightly in a wholly determined way; that such goods as sympathy and heroism have greater value if they are freely chosen; and that such evils as cruelty are 'necessary accompaniments' of freedom, just as pain is a logically necessary pre-condition of sympathy. Mackie disagrees. Theists believe that God made human beings such that they sometimes freely prefer what is good to what is evil: so why did he not make them such that 'they always freely choose the good'? There is no 'logical impossibility' in human beings freely choosing the good sometimes, so there is no logical obstacle to their always freely choosing it. God's choice was not between making innocent automata, or beings who, in acting freely, would sometimes go wrong. God could have created beings who would act freely, 'but always go right'. God's failure to avail himself of this option is inconsistent with his being 'both omnipotent and wholly good'.[4]

## IN DEFENCE OF GOD

### *A LOGICAL FLAW IN THE UTOPIA THESIS*

Ninian Smart challenges Mackie's 'Utopia thesis', that God could have created human beings who would always do what is right, on logical grounds. The assertion that God might have made human beings who were 'immunized from evil' is conceivable, and does not appear to be self-contradictory. But such ethical concepts as 'good', 'right', 'courageous' and 'generous' presuppose a fallible humanity, prone to wrongdoing. Yes, God might have created an alternative universe, in which human beings did not yield to temptation, but the 'usual criteria' for calling someone good (or bad) would not apply in such a world, because human beings would be programmed always to resist temptations successfully. Terms of moral approbation and disapprobation would be unintelligible; moral discourse, education and edification would be meaningless and purposeless; and human beings would not be genuinely free. Smart doubts whether this utopian alternative would actually be preferable to the world as it is.[5]

## THE BEST OF ALL POSSIBLE WORLDS, WHICH CANNOT BE OTHER THAN IT IS

Gottfried Leibniz accepts the full implications of the claim that an infinitely good and powerful God created the world. Despite appearances to the contrary, this must be the best of all possible worlds. God, '*the first reason of things*', is omnipotent and omnibenevolent, so his ideas include 'an infinity of other worlds'. As the best of all possible worlds is the only world that such a God would have created, there must be a sufficient reason for his choice of this particular one: 'if it were not the best (*optimum*) among all possible worlds, God would not have produced any'. Everything in the universe derives from God, and under his direction, and in accordance with the principle of plenitude, it contains the greatest possible order, variety and perfection, which would be imperilled if things were other than they are.

However, as such a God made the world, it is hard to understand why it contains evil and suffering. An omnipotent and all-loving God would have been expected to create a world containing none. Leibniz's insistence that the world is the best possible one makes this challenge even more acute, but he does not try to evade the issue; if God is an absolutely perfect being, it follows that he must always act in the most perfect way, both metaphysically and morally. Leibniz invents the term 'theodicy' to refer to his attempt to reconcile evil and suffering in the world with the Christian concept of God. Our knowledge of the general harmony of the universe, and the hidden reasons for God's conduct, is very limited, and our finite minds cannot comprehend God's infinite purposes. The best of all possible worlds does not mean a world with no evil, only a world containing less evil than any alternative one. Although it is beyond our understanding, the evil that exists in the world is absolutely necessary:

> if the smallest evil that comes to pass in the world were missing . . . it would no longer be this world; which, with nothing omitted and all allowance made, was found the best by the Creator who chose it.

Voltaire's sardonic response was to depict his Leibniz character, Dr Pangloss, as absurdly and unreasonably optimistic about the outcomes that the 'chain of events' in this, the 'best of all possible worlds', would produce, irrespective of the pain and suffering involved. Pangloss assures his student, Candide:

> if you had not been turned out of a beautiful mansion . . . if you had not been involved in the Inquisition . . . had not wandered over America on foot . . . had not . . . lost all those sheep . . . you would not be here eating candied fruit and pistachio nuts.

It is easy to scoff, but if there is a reality corresponding to the Christian concept of God, and this God made the world from nothing (*ex nihilo*), then it must be the best of all possible worlds. Yes, Philo suggests ways in which even limited human intelligence can restructure it, so as to cause less pain and suffering to its occupants. But Philo's perspective is that of a finite being; possessed of God's omniscience, he might see that the world as it is, with all its faults, actually is the best possible world.

For Leibniz's fellow rationalist philosopher, Baruch de Spinoza, this world, with its evil and suffering, is the only possible world. God is a necessary being, so:

> All things necessarily follow from the nature of God, and by the nature of God are conditioned to exist and act in a particular way.

People mistakenly 'assign to God . . . absolute free will', because they believe that God is free to produce, or not to produce, the things that flow from his nature. But, for the order of nature to be different, God's nature would also have to be different. God could not have created things other than they are, so the world has not been created to serve any plan or purpose. Ultimate reality just is as it is, eternally and necessarily, so everything that exists, including evil, pain and suffering, does so 'in the highest perfection, inasmuch as they have necessarily followed from a most perfect nature'.

For Spinoza, the problem of evil arises from human beings' refusal to accept reality. 'Ignorant of the causes of things', they have developed an anthropocentric and teleological view of the universe. They believe that everything in nature acts as they do themselves, 'with an end in view', and that, under the direction of God, who 'made all things for man', nature's purpose is to serve their needs. Instead of recognizing that 'nature has no particular goal', they account for the fact that misfortune affects the pious as badly as the impious by saying that 'God's judgments' are beyond human understanding. Such human explanations of nature 'are mere modes of imagining' and do not indicate 'the true nature of anything'.[6]

## THE PRINCIPLE OF PLENITUDE

We have referred to the Augustinian 'theodicy', which is an anachronism, as the term was not invented until the 17th century. But what is Augustine of Hippo's influential explanation of evil and suffering in the world? An important element is the principle of plenitude, which we have already come across in Leibniz's theodicy. For Augustine, the created order's richness and diversity reflect 'the goodness of God'. The problem is that parts of creation, such as fire, cold, wild animals, and so on, do not always 'suit the inadequacy and frailty of our mortal flesh'. Critics and heretics fail to recognize the role of all aspects of nature 'in the splendour of the providential order', and their invaluable contribution to it. Everything in nature can 'contribute to our benefit', provided we make proper use of it; for example, poisons can be made into medicines. Instead of complaining about aspects of creation which we do not understand, we must discover their purpose; if we cannot, we should accept that 'deficiency of insight' prevents us from doing so.

Augustine is emphatic that: 'there is no such entity in nature as "evil"'; it is merely *privatio boni*, the absence of good. This is not an assertion that pain and suffering do not occur in the world, but a metaphysical point about the nature of a world that has been created *ex nihilo* by an omnipotent and all-loving God. The world is intrinsically good, but, while God is 'unchangeable and completely incorruptible', creation is not. Made from nothing, it (human beings included) is finite, fallible and corruptible.

## THE INEVITABILITY OF SIN ENTERING THE WORLD

It is the corruptible nature of what has been made from 'nothing at all' that is the cause of sin, evil and suffering. Human beings sin simply because, unlike God's, theirs is a created and therefore corruptible nature. But, although it is 'a falling away' of his work, as God is omniscient, he foreknew that human beings would sin, and their doing so cannot upset his plan for his world; he will bring good 'out of man's evil'. For Augustine, the story of the Fall describes how corruptible human beings, personified in Adam and Eve, the first human beings, actually become corrupted. At creation, they are living in a perfect relationship with God, 'in a paradise both material and spiritual'. However, the personification of corrupted creation, Satan, having chosen to turn away from God, envies their 'unfallen condition' and worms his way into their consciousness. Eve and Adam succumb to temptation and disobey God, with devastating consequences:

> The effect of that sin was to subject human nature to all the process of decay which we see and feel . . . to death also . . . man was distracted and tossed . . . a very different being from what he was in paradise before his sin.

As obedience to God is the 'mother and guardian' of all the virtues of rational creatures, it was 'calamitous' for them to act according to their own will and not to obey their Creator. The unrighteousness of disobeying God's prohibition was all the greater, 'in proportion to the ease with which it could have been observed'. As sin has entered the world, and human beings are now disposed to sinning, Augustine tells us that we should think in terms of two cities, which have been created 'by two kinds of love'. The 'earthly city' is the result of 'self-love reaching the point of contempt for God'. However, in the 'Heavenly City', there is:

> the love of God carried as far as contempt of self . . . the earthly city glories in itself, the Heavenly City glories in the Lord . . . rightly worships the true God, and looks for its reward in the fellowship of the saints.[7]

While the personification of evil in the person of Satan is true to the Genesis story, it is regrettable in two respects. It establishes what seems to be a rival and opposing source of power to God in the world, the origin and existence of which is inexplicable. It also distracts attention from Augustine's key point, which is that what is finite, though it may be good, is corruptible, because, unlike God, it is created from nothing. Human beings do not need Satan's temptation to cause them to sin: moral corruption is the inevitable consequence of their finitude and corruptibility.

And, because of their finite nature, corruptibility and sinfulness, human beings not only often act wrongly and disobey God but also have a perverse tendency, as Isaiah of Jerusalem expresses it, to 'call evil good and good evil', to 'put darkness for light and light for darkness'. Moral imperatives may be clearly and unambiguously stated, yet human beings will twist them to suit their inclinations, and to justify their immoral actions, without even being aware that they have done so, or that the deeds they have performed are wholly at odds with the ethical principles they avow. In her account of the trial of the Nazi war criminal, Adolf Eichmann, Hannah Arendt describes how Eichmann claimed to have lived his whole life according to Kant's moral precepts and definition of duty, until given the task of carrying out the Final Solution, when 'he had ceased to live according to Kantian principles'. Arendt remarks that Eichmann had not simply dismissed Kantian morality:

> he had distorted it to read: Act as if the principle of your actions were the same as that of the legislator of the law of the land . . .'Act in such a way that the Furhrer, if he knew your action, would approve it'.[8]

## A VALE OF SOUL-MAKING, NOT PARADISE ON EARTH

John Hick traces his version of theodicy back to St Irenaeus, who regarded the world as having been designed by God as a vale of soul-making. Its purpose is to be an environment in which human beings may develop the more valuable qualities of moral personality, such as courage and compassion. Hick sums up the difference between his neo-Irenaean theodicy and Augustine's, thus:

> the Augustinian theodicy seeks its clue to the meaning of evil in the past, in a supposed Fall of man at the beginning of history . . . it is a mythological theodicy. The Irenaean view . . . looks to the future. It is eschatological, centring on the belief that in the end good will be triumphantly brought out of evil.

The obvious difference is that, while the Augustinian theodicy is negative, enshrining the view that God's finitely perfect world went wrong, for reasons which, despite Augustine's persuasive arguments, are not entirely clear, Hick's theodicy is positive. God designed the world like this because it actually *is* the best of all possible worlds for serving God's purpose as a vale of soul-making. Hick invites us to imagine the world as 'a paradise from which all possibility of pain and suffering were excluded'. No-one would ever be able to harm anyone else. Fraud, deceit, conspiracy and treason would always leave the fabric of society undamaged. There would be no point in concern for the welfare of others, as they would have no needs and face no dangers. Hick draws out the full implications of Smart's response to Mackie. In such a world, not only would our 'present ethical concepts' be meaningless, but, in this 'hedonistic paradise', there could be no such thing as a wrong or right action. Courage and fortitude would serve no purpose, as there would be no dangers or difficulties. Generosity, kindness, love and unselfishness, which presuppose life in a stable environment, could not be developed. However well it might promote pleasure, such a world would be ill-suited for developing 'the moral qualities of human personality'; it would be 'the worst of all possible worlds' for such a purpose.

Hick's Irenaean theodicy poses a formidable challenge to non-theists who seek to utilize the problem of evil and suffering as their most powerful argument against God's goodness – and existence. The world is as it is, not because it went wrong, as a result of human sin, but because this is how God designed it for his particular purpose. The world's defects and difficulties are a necessary condition of the moral development of creatures fit for ultimate fellowship with their creator:

> Instead of regarding man as having been created by God in a finished state, as a finitely perfect being fulfilling the divine intention . . . and then falling disastrously away from this . . . man . . . is only the raw material for a further . . . stage of God's creative work. This is the leading of men as relatively free . . . persons . . . towards that quality of personal existence that is the finite likeness of God.

There are problems with this type of theodicy. It presupposes human freewill, the existence of which determinists deny. Unless human beings are genuinely free to respond to the challenges they face, and capable of developing moral qualities in response to them, the exercise would be pointless and cruel. It is wholly speculative. It assumes belief in an all-powerful and all-loving God, and then tries to find a way of reconciling this concept of God with the world's evil and suffering. Surely, such a God could have made a world containing many of the tests that develop human beings' moral qualities, but without such appalling extremes of human suffering?[9]

## WHAT MAKES THE BEST POSSIBLE WORLD

Pain and suffering affect both theists and non-theists, but with the key difference that, for theists, the best possible world will be one that serves God's purpose. Many Christians accept that, in order to fulfil its role as a place of 'soul-making', in preparation for eternal life with God, the world has to be as it is. For non-theists, the best possible world will be one that fulfils the utilitarian goal of minimizing suffering and maximizing happiness, so, if God made it, his handiwork falls short of what they would expect a (all-) powerful and (all-) loving God to have created. They will regard theodicies as ingenious, but ultimately unconvincing, attempts to reconcile belief in a particular concept of God with the undeniable fact of the world's evil and suffering. The problem does not arise, or arises less acutely, if the concept of God is changed from one who is infinitely powerful and infinitely good to one who is either infinitely powerful or infinitely good, or whose power and love are finite. In Chapter 2, we saw that one of the central projects of natural theology, to establish God's existence and nature, through rational arguments based on human experience of the world, is unachievable. The problem of evil is another reason why such an enterprise is doomed to failure.

## THROUGH THE INCARNATION, GOD SHARES OUR SUFFERING

The philosophical-theologian is concerned not only with the 'why' of the problem of evil and suffering but also with the 'how' of theists' response to it in their lives. Christianity's main symbols, the cross and the crucifix (a cross with Jesus impaled upon it), tell us that suffering is at the heart of Christianity: the central Christian belief is that Jesus of Nazareth, Christianity's founder, was both a human being and God-incarnate, and that, through his life and death, God shares the human experience of suffering. Fully human and fully divine, Jesus suffered an agonizing death for our sakes and our salvation, and then, having risen from the dead, thus triumphing over death, offers us eternal life, despite our sins, provided we have faith in God and the salvific work wrought through Jesus. St Paul declares that we are:

> justified by his grace as a gift, through the redemption which is in Christ Jesus, whom God put forward as an expiation by his blood to be received by faith . . . he justifies him who has faith in Jesus.

Every Sunday, Christians affirm these core beliefs when they repeat the Apostles' Creed, declaring that Jesus is God's:

> only Son our Lord, Who was conceived by the Holy Ghost, Born of the Virgin Mary, Suffered under Pontius Pilate, Was crucified, dead, and buried: He descended into hell; The third day he rose again from the dead; He ascended into heaven, And sitteth on the right hand of God the Father Almighty.

These statements raise questions about what the belief that Jesus was God's 'only Son' means; how a God-incarnate could have suffered at all; the purpose of Jesus' suffering and death and how it leads to hope of salvation and eternal life; and what is meant by the claim that Jesus 'atoned' for the sins of human beings.[10]

The main interest of Paul and the early Christians was not in definitions of Jesus' divine sonship, but in their certainty that he was the Saviour, 'who gave himself for our sins . . . according to the will of our God the Father'. However, as disputes raged in the Early Church about this issue and what it meant to believe that God is a Trinity of Father, Son and Holy Spirit, greater precision was necessary. In the Nicene Creed, adopted by the Christian Church in 325 CE, Jesus is described as 'the only-begotten Son of God', who is 'of one substance with the Father'. But establishing Jesus' divine status, by using the philosophical concepts of the era, as well as creating new problems, highlights the issue of how 'the only-begotten Son of God' could really have suffered. Indeed, how could he be human at all, despite the Nicene Creed's insistence that: 'he became incarnate by the Holy Spirit and the virgin Mary, and was made human'?[11]

In his account of Jesus' trial, crucifixion and death, St Mark depicts Jesus as undergoing severe mental anguish, as well as acute physical suffering. After the Last Supper, Jesus knows that he is a marked man, who is going to be betrayed by Judas Iscariot, and that his time is running out. Mark does not minimize Jesus' fear and anxiety, describing him as increasingly 'distressed and troubled', admitting to his disciples that: 'My soul is very sorrowful, even to death'. Jesus prays to God to spare him the terrible ordeal he faces, but accepts God's decision, whatever it is:

> Abba, Father, all things are possible to thee; remove this cup from me; yet not what I will, but what thou wilt.

After his trial, prior to which his disciples have abandoned or denied him, he was crucified between two robbers, and subjected to the ridicule of onlookers, who taunt him with such jibes as: 'He saved others; he cannot save himself'. Even those being crucified with him join in the general mockery. In agony, alone, deserted by his disciples, betrayed and humiliated, Jesus, before his death, cries out despairingly, 'My God, my God, why hast thou forsaken me?'.[12]

Mark could not have conveyed the reality of Jesus' human suffering more vividly, but one of the heresies that afflicted the Early Christian Church was Docetism ('appearance-ism'), which denied

Jesus' humanity. Christ may have appeared to be 'tangible flesh and blood', but 'he was pure spirit', his physical appearance a 'mere semblance'. But if Jeus' humanity was an appearance, so, too, was his suffering, casting doubt on Christianity's central teaching, that Jesus, as God-incarnate, endured the agonies of crucifixion, in order to redeem humanity. The Church needed to develop the Nicene doctrine in a way that put both Jesus' humanity and his divinity beyond doubt.

In 451 CE, the Chalcedonian Definition was agreed, which declared Jesus to be, at once 'truly God and truly man', of 'one substance with the Father as regards his Godhead . . . of one substance with us as regards his manhood'. Though these two natures, the divine and the human, were united in Jesus, neither was negated or compromised by the other:

> the characteristics of each nature . . . coming together to form one person . . . not as parted or separated into two persons, but one and the same Son and Only-begotten God the Word, Lord Jesus Christ.

The Chalcedonian Definition attempts to define the indefinable; it stretches words and theological terminology to breaking-point, in order to give verbal expression to the mystery of the incarnation, and what it means for one and the same person to be both divine and human. However, the essential message is clear: Jesus is both God and man. When he laid down his life 'for us men and for our salvation', his suffering was as real as that of any other human being subjected to crucifixion.[13]

## JESUS' RESURRECTION AND THE TRIUMPH OVER DEATH

Resurrection and triumph quickly follow death and despair. Two days after the crucifixion, Jesus appears to Mary Magdalene, after she and other women have visited his tomb and found that the stone has been rolled away. The frightened apostles do not believe her story, but Jesus appears to them, and rebukes them for their 'unbelief and hardness of heart'. He explains the meaning and significance of his death and resurrection, which offer universal hope and salvation. Their mission is to preach the gospel to 'the whole creation'; those who believe and are baptized will be saved, those who do not 'will be condemned'. Inspired and succoured by the ascended Jesus, 'they went forth and preached everywhere'.[14]

## ATONING FOR OUR SINS

In some sense, Jesus' death has 'atoned' for human sin. Salvation and eternal life are freely available to human beings, on condition that they have faith in Jesus. In Romans 5, Paul gives further explanation of what 'atonement' means:

> since we are justified by faith, we have peace with God through our Lord Jesus Christ. Through him we have obtained access to this grace in which we stand, and we rejoice in our hope of sharing the glory of God.

God's love for his creatures is so great that Jesus Christ, God-incarnate, died for us. 'while we were yet sinners'. Inevitably (and an obstacle to understanding the atonement today), Paul falls back on the sacrificial language that was familiar to his readers. As we are 'justified' by Jesus' blood, we will be 'saved by him from the wrath of God'; through Jesus' death, 'we are reconciled' to God. Paul contrasts Adam's disobedience of God with Jesus' obedience:

> If, because of one man's trespass, death reigned . . . much more will those who receive the abundance of grace and the free gift of righteousness reign in life through the one man Jesus Christ.

This does not mean that, in this world, Christians will enjoy an easy life. They will suffer for their beliefs, as Jesus did. But, knowing that 'Christ died for the ungodly', and with God's love 'poured into our hearts through the Holy Spirit', they must rejoice in their sufferings, which will develop their resilience and endurance.[15]

So, are we to believe that God, in and through Jesus, made a sacrifice of himself to himself, and gave 'satisfaction' to himself, so that the debt of human sin could be paid off? Paul's sacrificial language is off-putting. The idea of sinful humanity being 'justified' by Jesus' blood, and therefore 'saved by him from the wrath of God', seems barbaric. Elsewhere, Paul refers to Jesus as the 'one mediator between God and men', who gave himself 'as a ransom for all', through whom 'we have redemption' and forgiveness of sins. But what is the point of it all? If God is going to forgive us, why not simply do so, without going through the rigmarole of the incarnation, crucifixion and resurrection? It does not seem to fit in with what we would expect from a loving God.[16]

It is helpful to look at how a previous generation of philosophical-theologians tried to make the issue comprehensible. In a series of open lectures, delivered during the Second World War, when interest in Christian teaching was particularly strong, J.S. Whale warned his listeners against paying too much heed to 'the technical language of theology'. In the context of the atonement, terms like 'propitiation', 'expiation', 'ransom' do 'more harm than good'. All we need to understand about the atonement is that 'Christ dies for our sins' and that the crucifixion is 'the supreme manifestation of the redeeming love of God'. In the late 1950s, Joseph Haroutian accepted that 'orthodox "satisfaction theories"' no longer appealed to Christians: they viewed the idea of God's anger with his creatures being 'appeased by the sufferings and death of the Son of God', with disfavour. Recent emphasis was on the 'sacrificial love' that Jesus showed for sinful humanity, and on his continuing 'moral influence' as an example that Christians can follow in their own lives. John A.T. Robinson, addressing the increasingly post-Christian society of the early 1970s, highlights the 'gap between doctrine and experience'. Christianity is a living religion, which must preach the 'great existential realities' of God's love to today's world. As traditionally conceived, the atonement, which is actually about God's continuing and inexhaustible love for humanity, expressed through the life and death of Jesus, and 'the transformation of human relationships here and now', appears to be about a 'distant divine-human transaction on "a green hill far away"'.

These insights are as valid today as when they were written. We must not allow the archaic, biblical language of sacrifice and satisfaction to obscure the meaning of the atonement, or to make us think that its purpose is the appeasement of God's wrath against sinful humanity, rather than the all-important expression of God's love for his creatures. Although Jesus' crucifixion took place in Palestine, over two thousand years ago, the process of what William Temple called 'universal redemption', which flows from it, goes on 'here and now'. T.E. Jessop rightly reminds us that, when 'we think of Christ's death as a sacrifice *to* God . . . it was also a sacrifice *by* God', a point we tend to overlook, through thinking of the incarnation and the atonement as discrete doctrines, when they are interlocking ones. Jessop is also right to deprecate any hope of finding a wholly satisfactory formulation of the doctrine of the atonement:

> Through His dying, Christ became not only the revealer of God's concern, but also the means by which that concern is able to move savingly to those who believe Him to be that revelation and that means. Exactly how His death is that means is a question that belongs to theological theorising.[17]

## CHRISTIANITY TEACHES HOW TO RESPOND TO EVIL AND SUFFERING

When we discuss the problem of evil and suffering, we are prone to what might be called 'the Benthamite fallacy', the tendency to think of both pleasure and pain quantitively, and to assess the state of the world by trying to measure, on a crude, mental 'felicific calculus', the total quantities of pleasure and happiness, versus pain and suffering, that it contains. C.S. Lewis warns us against making the problem of pain and suffering worse than it is, by vague talk about the 'unimaginable sum of human misery', which does not actually exist. He asks us to imagine two patients in a dentist's waiting-room, each with a 'toothache of intensity x'. We could say that 'the total amount of pain in the room is now 2x', but neither patient actually suffers 2x. And that 'composite pain' never afflicts anyone, because there is no 'sum of suffering'. The maximum that a single person can suffer is terrible, but it is the maximum of suffering there can ever be in the universe. The addition of 'a million fellow-sufferers adds no more pain'. So, when Jesus suffered and died in agony on the cross, for the sake of sinful humanity, he endured all the pain that anyone in the world, at any point in history, can ever experience.[18]

For many Christians, the role of religion is not to explain or justify the presence of evil and suffering in the world, but to show human beings how to deal with it. They believe that, through Jesus, who embodied and revealed in his life on earth God's infinite love for human beings, and who died on the cross on their behalf, God has brought about human beings' salvation. Although disobedience and sin opened up a gulf between God and humanity, Jesus' death and resurrection effected an 'atonement' or reconciliation. They believe that they should follow the example of Jesus, who spent his life on earth helping others, and use Jesus' ethical teachings as a blueprint for living a life that reflects God's *agape* for them. They trust that God has an ultimate purpose for them, so that eternal life will follow physical death:

> the Christian response to suffering has always been as much practical as theoretical. . . . The practical response of Christianity arises directly out of the belief that in the life of Christ God has set his mark on the world . . . The life of Christ is not usually claimed to dissolve or even explain the realities of suffering, but it becomes for Christians an essential element in their response . . . in the worst agony there remains something which is not destroyed, and which gives grounds, if not for explanation, at least for assurance and hope.

And perhaps, for Christians, experience of suffering is actually an indispensable prerequisite of an adequate response to Christ, who, though he was in 'the form of God, did not count equality with God a thing to be grasped', but 'emptied himself', and, 'being born in the likeness of men', became 'obedient unto death, even death on a cross'. Edith Stein (St Teresa Benedicta of the Cross) maintains that, while 'No searching human spirit can penetrate the unfathomable mystery of the dying God-man's abandonment by God', those who follow in Christ's footsteps, though they will experience the 'extreme bitterness' of this abandonment, will also discover through it, 'union with the Crucified'. Like the Spanish mystic, St John of the Cross, they will find that, 'the soul comes to true self-knowledge and to enlightenment about God's immeasurable greatness and holiness precisely through the experience of her own nothingness and impotence in the dark night' of suffering. And, as Marilyn McCord Adams rightly points out, this view of evil and suffering is probably comprehensible only to Christians and theists, because it involves insights and values which non-believers simply do not share:

> perhaps our deepest suffering as much as our highest joys may themselves be direct visions into the inner life of God. . . . And if a face-to-face vision of God is a good for humans incommensurate with any non-transcendent goods or ills, so any vision of God (including horrendous suffering) would have a good aspect in so far as it is a vision of God (even if it has an evil aspect in so far as it is horrendous suffering).[19]

## MIRACLES, PRAYER AND PROVIDENCE

### *YES, CHRISTIANS DO BELIEVE THAT JESUS PERFORMED MIRACLES*

A miracle is an event which cannot be accounted for according to established laws of nature, which it appears to break, and which is attributed to God or supernatural causes. The Gospels contain many examples of Jesus performing miracles; and if, as Christians believe, he is God-incarnate, there is no reason to doubt his power to do so. On the other hand, Christians believe that God made the world as a stable environment, which operates in a predictable way, according to general scientific laws. If God interferes with the normal operation of the universe, he is disrupting the working of his own creation, which seems improbable. Again, the New Testament was written two thousand years ago, in a pre-scientific era. Perhaps the accounts of Jesus' miracles reflect the misinterpretations and exaggerations of an ignorant and credulous age. If we had been there, with the benefit of our greater scientific knowledge, would we have interpreted and described the events rather differently? Jesus' miracles are not all of the same sort; many are miracles of healing, which show Jesus' compassion for the sick and the suffering. But we will start by considering two of his more problematic 'nature-miracles', in which Jesus demonstrates power over nature and the ability to set aside general scientific laws.

After a busy day of preaching, Jesus and his disciples set out for the opposite shore of the Sea of Galilee. A great storm blows up, and their boat begins to fill with water. Alarmed, the disciples wake a sleeping Jesus: does he not care that they all going to perish? Jesus' unflustered response is to order wind and sea to be still, and the storm to subside. He upbraids the disciples for their fear and lack of faith. They are awe-stricken that 'even wind and sea obey him'. On another occasion, Jesus seeks out a 'lonely place', where he and his disciples can rest. However, eager crowds follow him, and he preaches to them. Towards the end of the day, Jesus' disciples urge him to send the 'great throng' to find food. They are astonished when Jesus tells them to feed the crowd themselves; there is no food and not enough money to buy any. Jesus asks them to find out how much food the crowd has. It turns out to be five loaves and two fish. Jesus orders the crowd to sit down in groups, looks up to heaven, blesses and breaks the loaves and fishes and gives them to his disciples to distribute among the five thousand people present. Mark tells us that not only was there sufficient food to satisfy the huge crowd, but afterwards they collected 'twelve baskets full of broken pieces and of the fish'.

Jesus' healing-miracles have the obvious purpose of curing illness and relieving suffering. But do the nature-miracles have any worthwhile purpose? St Mark appears to present these and the other nature-miracles simply as demonstrations of Jesus' miraculous power. Five thousand people were fed, but they do not seem to have been literally starving. And was there any point in Jesus stilling a storm? To the gospel-writers, and to generations of Christians since, it does matter that Jesus is able to feed 5,000 people, and quell a mighty storm: nature itself is bearing witness to his divine status. Also important is the effect that Jesus' presence and words have on his disciples: their faith in, and response to, him inspires them with confidence and subdues their fear.

What about the healing-miracles? At beginning of his ministry, when Jesus is teaching in a Capernaum synagogue, he is confronted by a man with an 'unclean spirit', then believed to be a common cause of both mental and physical illness, who recognizes him as 'the Holy One of God'. The onlookers are amazed when Jesus cures the man, commenting on the 'authority' with which he 'commands even the unclean spirits'. After curing Simon's mother-in-law of a fever, and an evening of healing all those brought to him, 'who were sick or possessed with demons', Jesus rose early and went to a lonely place to pray. Later, when a leper begs to be healed, Jesus is 'moved with pity', and does so. His return to Capernaum is widely reported, and large crowds gather at the house where he is staying, to hear his preaching. Four men carry a paralytic man there, but the crowd prevents them approaching Jesus. They make a hole in the roof, and lower the man into the room where Jesus is. Seeing 'their faith', Jesus tells the paralytic, 'My son, your sins are forgiven'. These words provoke an angry reaction from some of those present, who condemn Jesus' words as blasphemy; only God can forgive sins. But Jesus asks them: is it easier to say, 'Your sins are forgiven' or 'Rise, take up your pallet and walk'? However, to show his 'authority on earth to forgive sins', he tells the paralytic to take up his pallet and go home, which, to the crowd's amazement, he does.

Is this how it happened? Did Jesus perform these and many other miracles? We have to decide for ourselves. In all the accounts of Jesus' miracles, we should note the emphasis on faith and prayer; individual and group responses to Jesus' personality, spiritual power and authority; the forgiveness of sins as part of the healing process; and Jesus' compassion for the sick and suffering. Obviously, if Jesus was God-incarnate, in whom 'the whole fullness of deity dwells bodily', he had the divine authority and power to perform miracles. Even the most sceptical reader of the Gospel narratives cannot dismiss Jesus as a mere wonderworker; the miracles he performed are an integral part of the life and work of an exceptional spiritual leader, with a profound awareness of God and of his own divine mission.[20]

## THE CASE AGAINST MIRACLES

### *THEY ARE CONTRARY TO OUR EXPERIENCE OF THE WORLD . . .*

David Hume's central objection to miracles is that they are contrary to what we have observed about how the world works. A miracle would be 'a violation of the laws of nature', which have been formulated on the basis of uniform human experience. The fact that a miracle would breach a law of nature, and cause it to cease to be one, is a 'direct and full *proof*' against it. Attributing a miracle to God does not make its occurrence more probable, as we have no knowledge of God. Hume suggests a test, against which any miracle claim should be measured: it should not be believed, unless its non-occurrence would be 'more miraculous' than the miracle itself'. It is hard to see how such a test could be applied objectively. Inveterate sceptics about miracles would always deny their occurrence, as Hume's comments about the miracles described in the Old Testament indicate. He maintains that the 'falsehood' of such a book, full of 'prodigies and miracles', and produced by an ignorant people, whose view of the world is very different from the modern one, seems less unlikely than the miracles it relates.

By this point, Hume has moved from logical argument to invective. He insists that accounts of miracles always originate 'among ignorant and barbarous nations'; have never been attested by enough people of integrity to prove they are true; and that human beings are generally too inclined to throw aside common sense when told of something 'utterly absurd and miraculous'. He also maintains that accounts of miracles in one religion should be treated as contradicting those of other religions, although this would only be a valid point if the truth-claims of one religion are regarded as excluding those of others. Hume observes (disingenuously, in view of his religious scepticism) that it is the 'continued miracle' of faith that enables believers to accept the teachings of Christianity, not reason, nor (we must conclude) accounts of miracles that are unlikely to have occurred.

Patrick Nowell-Smith, who agrees with Hume, highlights the faulty reasoning of theists who fail to distinguish between the claim that an occurrence cannot be explained in terms of 'natural agents', and the further claim that it must therefore be 'ascribed to supernatural agents'. Even if it is accepted that 'extraordinary phenomena occur', there is no proof that God causes them. However, if theists are culpable for their over-eagerness in attributing unusual events to a divine cause, so is Hume in his total refusal to accept the possibility of miracles. We might adapt the question Flew directs at theists, and put it to Hume: what would have to happen to force him, not just 'morally and wrongly', but 'logically and rightly', to admit that miracles may occur. Let us imagine that Hume had been present at the Feeding of the Five Thousand. He would have preferred to tear his eyes out, rather than admit that they were beholding a miracle. As William Barclay rightly observes, this dismissive approach to accounts of miracles, which rules them out on the basis of their being 'impossible', is both illogical and unscientific:

> miracles are a matter of *evidence*. . . the more unusual a thing is, the better must be the evidence before we can accept it; but if the evidence for an 'impossible' thing is strong enough, then the thing must be accepted as having happened, 'impossible' or 'not'.[21]

## . . . APPEAL TO THE IGNORANT MASSES, AND ARE UNNECESSARY ANYWAY

Hume's refusal to countenance miracles, or God as a possible cause of events in the world, is also hard to reconcile with his radically empiricist view of causality, which holds that the popular belief that certain causes and effects are necessarily connected is not based on any actual impression of a necessary connexion between them. What we observe is that one event (A) regularly follows another event (B). But in this 'succession of objects', there is nothing to suggest a 'necessary connexion'. It is therefore rather surprising that, when it comes to miracles, Hume appears to be so rigidly attached to the unvarying operation of natural laws, which are mere generalizations about how the world operates, based on observation and experience. If there is no 'necessary connexion' between a particular cause and a particular effect, there is no good reason why, on some occasions, as when miracles occur, God should not operate as a causal factor.

To make a convincing objection to miracles along these lines, a rather different view of the world and how it works is required. Baruch de Spinoza agrees with Hume that the ignorant masses love miracles. They call divine anything that 'transcends human understanding', and of which the cause is unknown. They believe that

God's power is revealed by extraordinary events, and that the clearest possible proof of God's existence arises when nature seems to break 'her accustomed order'. They call these phenomena miracles and, out of piety and in defiance of scientific knowledge, choose to marvel at things that they do not understand.

However, Spinoza is entitled to make this argument because he does not share Hume's view of the universe. He believes that whatever happens in the world happens according to 'the fixed and immutable order of nature'. As the 'laws of nature are decrees of God, following from the necessity and perfection of the Divine nature', miracles are impossible, because they would 'contravene the divine Decree', and mean that God was acting against his own nature. For Spinoza, every event which is described in the scriptures must actually have happened naturally and necessarily, and anything that appears to contravene nature must have been 'foisted into the sacred writings'. The object of the Bible is not to convince the reason, but to capture the imagination. However, when properly understood, the miracles described in it will be seen to be natural occurrences that comply with natural laws.

But does religion even need miracles? Immanuel Kant argues that Christianity is primarily concerned with obeying the moral law and treating human duties as divine commands:

> Apart from a good life-conduct, anything which the human being supposes that he can do to become well-pleasing to God is mere religious delusion and counterfeit service of God.

Kant does not deny the occurrence of miracles, and, when a religion like Christianity, which prioritizes high moral standards, replaces one in which cultic practices and ritual observances have had a key role, miracles may help to gain acceptance for the moral religion, even when it can hold its own 'on rational grounds'. And there is no need to challenge 'narratives and interpretations' involving miracles, or people's belief in them. God is the world's ruler and creator, according to both 'the order of nature as well as the moral order'. If, in 'special cases', God allows nature to deviate from the natural order, and miracles to occur, human beings know that they always do so in accordance with 'the *general moral* law that whatever God does will all be good'.[22]

## IN DEFENCE OF MIRACLES

### *THE STRONG PRESUMPTION AGAINST MIRACLES IS NOT JUSTIFIED . . .*

Joseph Butler wonders why there is such a strong presumption against miracles. We believe that, because nature usually operates predictably, according to general laws, it must always do so, but there are many irregularities in nature that we do not understand. We should think of miracles in terms of such 'extraordinary phenomena of nature' as comets or the existence of electricity. There would be a strong presumption against these if human beings were only familiar with the ordinary course of nature. If God does reveal himself to human beings, that revelation is likely to include events such as miracles, which 'afford mankind instruction additional to that of nature, and . . . attest to the truth of it'.

Richard Swinburne suggests that we should expect God to 'make his presence known to men', which may involve miraculous interruptions to the world's normal operation. Christianity's central message is of God's decisive intervention in the world, through the 'life, death and Resurrection of Jesus of Nazareth', in order to redeem human beings and reconcile them to himself. Jesus' life was full of miracles, and Christians regard 'these remarkable events' as evidence both of God's activity in the world and of his existence. To deny miracles, and therefore God's intervention in the natural order, is to elevate creation above its creator. It is to say that because God made a stable environment for human beings, which generally works in a predictable way, he cannot interfere with its operation. Yet, 'if natural laws operate because God makes them operate', then God is also able to suspend their operation, so 'the occurrence of the occasional violation . . . is . . . to be expected'.[23]

## . . . AND GOD'S INTERVENTION IN THE WORLD IS PART OF THE NATURAL ORDER

C.S. Lewis' interpretation of miracles answers many of the objections to them. If there is a 'Power outside Nature', the universe's normal operation, according to 'fixed laws', need not rule out 'supernatural interferences'. This would only be the case if the laws of nature were necessary and inevitable (as Spinoza contends that they are), but they are not. They are descriptive, not prescriptive: generalizations, based on human observation, about what events will occur, given the presence of certain causal factors. Divine intervention merely introduces a new causal factor, 'the activity of God', into the normal operation of the world, which produces a different outcome from the one that would have occurred, if it had not been present.

Therefore, miracles do not break laws of nature, as 'Nature digests or assimilates' the additional (divine) causal factor. In the case of the Virgin Birth, for example, if 'God creates a miraculous spermatozoon in the body of a virgin', no law of nature is broken. The additional causal factor is simply accommodated in the natural process, so that pregnancy follows in the normal way, and a child is born nine months later. Thus, a miracle is 'not an event without a cause or without results'. It is caused by God's activity; its results follow according to the laws of nature, and it interlocks with future events. The difference is that it does not interlock retrospectively with 'previous history'. So, God's intervention in the world may produce miraculous outcomes, which would not otherwise have occurred, but it is nonetheless 'natural' for them to do so: God's action is simply an additional causal factor in an event taking place in the world which he created.[24]

## WHY SHOULD WE PRAY?

### *BECAUSE JESUS PRAYED, AND TAUGHT HIS FOLLOWERS HOW TO PRAY . . .*

Jesus prayed often, and he is explicit about its efficaciousness. When his disciples are unable to heal a boy with 'a dumb spirit', he is brought to Jesus, who commands the spirt to 'come out of him'; the boy is cured. Later, the disciples question Jesus about their own inability to cast the spirit out, and he explains: 'This kind cannot be driven out by anything but prayer'. As we have seen, Jesus prayed intensely before his arrest, and it was through prayer that he was able to obey God and accept his own death. He taught his disciples that prayer is communication with God, not an opportunity for a public display of affected piety to impress onlookers. Whereas religious hypocrites pray in synagogues and public places, where 'they may be seen', the disciples must follow his example and pray 'to your Father who is in secret'. They must not 'heap up empty phrases', but use what is now known as 'The Lord's Prayer', addressing God as 'Our Father', and praying for the coming of God's kingdom, their daily bread, forgiveness of their wrongdoing, and help in resisting temptation and behaving forgivingly towards others.[25]

## ... AND WHEN CHRISTIANS PRAY, THEY SEEM TO EXPECT THEIR PRAYERS TO BE ANSWERED

Praying is a major part of Christian worship and private devotion. The Lord's Prayer is repeated at every Christian service, and, whether they are praying individually or collectively, Christians know that when they pray, they are communicating with God, and that their prayers must be sincere and unostentatious. However, the key question is: what exactly do Christians think they are doing, when they pray? The Lord's Prayer asks for God's help in providing what is necessary for survival ('our daily bread') and assistance with leading a Christian life, in the hope and expectation of the coming of God's kingdom. We might describe these as general requests, which relate to all human beings. But are these actually requests at all? They do not sound like a drowning person begging assistance from someone on the riverbank, or an application for a loan. They are more like someone, who is facing a challenge, asking for his family's and friends' moral support. In the *Collect for Grace*, what is sought from God is guidance to prevent the petitioners from falling into sin, and so to strengthen them that they 'do always that is righteous in thy sight'. The *Prayer of Saint Chrysostom* refers to God granting petitioners' requests, but only as God judges 'most expedient'. Yet, in intercessory prayers, Christians seek from God special providences or interventions in the world: to cure illness, for example. While the petitioner accepts that the decision is God's, such words as, 'if it shall be thy good pleasure to restore *him* to *his* former health', are unambiguous about petitioners' belief in God's power to grant the request.

Maurice Wiles, acknowledging that Christians have always prayed 'with the utmost regularity', considers that appeals to God for special providences or interferences in the world show misunderstanding of the nature of God's creative act:

> God's fundamental act . . . is the bringing into existence of the world. That is a continuous process, and every part of it is therefore in the broadest sense an expression of divine activity . . . God's love is shown in the fact that the world that he is bringing into being is designed to elicit a fullness of personal life through the exercise of freedom.

So, God's involvement with the world and human beings is confined to general providence, by which he 'upholds and sustains them in being', and guides the evolution of his creation as an environment in which his human creatures can develop their personalities freely. Particular providences are ruled out, because they would interfere with this process. Instead of looking (and praying) for 'particular divine acts', human beings should use their freedom, in this God-given environment, to grasp God's intention for creation, and, through prayer and reflection, learn how to respond to him fully and appropriately.[26]

## I AND THOU – THE HUMAN RELATIONSHIP WITH A PERSONAL GOD

While Wiles' Humean analysis removes some of the difficulties associated with prayer and providence, such as why God appears to answer some prayers, and help some petitioners, but not others, it not only fails to do justice to what Christians (believe they) are doing when they pray but also seems to deny major elements of Christian teaching. If we accept Spinoza's metaphysics, then there is no point in intercessory prayer: God cannot intervene to change events in the world, because everything that happens flows necessarily from his nature. But Christians do not agree with Spinoza. The essence of Christianity is that God intervened decisively in the world, through Jesus' incarnation, death and resurrection, in order to redeem human beings. Jesus prayed frequently, and the Gospels, the Epistles, and subsequent Christian testimony is of prayers being answered. For Christians, God is not a just a remote, transcendent being, but a personal God, a loving Father, 'who sent his only Son into the world that we might live through him'.

In his influential study of prayer, Friedrich Heiler identifies the three key elements of the prayer-experience as:

> faith in a living personal God, faith in His real, immediate presence, and a realistic fellowship into which man enters with a God conceived as present.

In Christianity, prayer is the turning of one person to another, to whom they open their heart in the language 'of an "I" to a "Thou"'. Martin Buber sees this 'I-Thou' relationship as crucial to our understanding of God. We may be 'incapable of declaring what God's essential being is', but we do know that, like ourselves, 'God is also a Person', who relates directly to his creatures through 'creative, revealing and redeeming acts'. So, when Christians pray to God, they believe that they are not only communicating with a transcendent being, but also with a Person, who hears their prayers and is able to grant their requests. But he will do so in the way that is 'most expedient for them'. And to those who portray the actual process pf praying as pointless, because an omniscient God will know the petitioner's requests before they have been uttered or even thought ('your Father knows what you need before you ask him'), perhaps we should recognize the importance of actually placing our needs and wants before God as Person, as we do with human persons. Luke's Gospel shows Jesus' disciples asking Jesus to teach them how to pray, 'as John taught his disciples'. But why did he wait to be asked? Why not volunteer the guidance? As Eleanore Stump pertinently observes:

> Perhaps the Gospel means us to understand that Jesus does so just in order to teach by experience as well as by sermon what is implicit throughout the Lord's Prayer: that asking makes a difference.[27]

## THE PARABLE OF THE GARDEN AND THE ILLATIVE SENSE

For non-theists, belief in miracles, prayer and divine providence may seem absurd. Yet, many religious people believe in all of them, through direct experience, trusted testimony or acceptance of their church's teaching and tradition. We have looked at arguments for and against these religious phenomena, which, at a purely intellectual level, are not conclusive for either side. For a variety of reasons, which may include upbringing, education, individual experience, personal relationships, exposure to religion and a host of other factors, some people are theists and others are not. Religious faith is a particular way of looking at the world. Theists do not see a different world; rather, they see the same world, but their perception of it, and of its origin, nature and value, is very different from that of non-theists.

This difference of perception is brought out in John Wisdom's 'Parable of the Gardener'. Two people (R1 and R2) return to their 'long-neglected garden' and find plants growing among the weeds. R1 says that a gardener must have been tending it, but nobody has seen a gardener. R1 then says that the gardener must have worked at night, but R2 says that a gardener would have cared for the plants better. Further searches reveal some evidence that a gardener may have been at work, but also of neglect. Each assembles exactly the same data about their own and other gardens, but still they cannot agree. Their different views about their garden reflect no difference in what they have found in their garden, or would find, if they searched it again. The 'gardener hypothesis has ceased to be experimental'. Their opposing positions indicate no difference in what they expect to discover about the garden now or in the future. However, despite the fact that neither expects anything of the garden that the other does not, their different beliefs about their garden, and the work of an invisible gardener in it, are accompanied by different feelings towards it.

As with the gardener hypothesis, so with the assertion of God's existence: it begins as an explanatory hypothesis, about the world and its existence, and it appears to be testable. In fact, it is not, but acceptance or rejection of the theistic assertion reflects and engenders very different perceptions and valuations of the world – whether it is simply a 'brute fact', which has evolved from matter, and operates according to general scientific laws, or whether it is God's creation, in which miracles occur, divine providence is a causal factor, and prayers are answered.[28]

The theist and the atheist have made up their minds. Let us expand Wisdom's parable to include a third returnee (R3), who participates in the searches, but is left sitting on the garden-fence, in a state of agnosticism. He has no settled pro- or anti-gardener, theistic or non-theistic, perception. Will he be able to make up his mind? R3 might ponder John Henry Newman's thoughts about what he calls 'The Illative Sense', that is, the human power of 'judging and concluding'. Newman's point is that, in empirical and practical matters, we do not reach our conclusions at the end of a process of syllogistic reasoning. After considering 'the nature and circumstances of the particular case', and assessing 'the cumulation of probabilities', we may judge that we have sufficient reasons for reaching a conclusion, even though we do not have absolute proof of it. Newman suggests that this is how we should approach religious questions. Such 'converging probabilities' as evidence of design in the universe and the operation of conscience suffice to justify the conclusion that God exists, and that he is a God who answers prayers and intervenes in the world. Newman is inviting R3 to recognize that life has a religious dimension, even though there is no absolute, objective proof of it. Of course, R3 may refuse the invitation.[29]

## NOTES

1 Hume, *Dialogues,* 63; Robinson, *An Atheists' Values*, 123–124; Flew and MacIntyre, *New Essays in Philosophical Theology*, 96–99.
2 Hume, *Dialogues,* 58–76.
3 Mill, *Three Essays on Religion*, 28–38, *Utilitarianism*, 21–22.
4 Pike, *God and Evil*, 55–56.
5 Pike, *God and Evil*, 103–112.
6 Leibniz, *Theodicy*, 38–39; Voltaire, *Candide*, 144; Spinoza, *Ethics*, 204–215
7 Augustine, *City of God*, 453–454, 568–71, 593–594.
8 Isaiah 5:7; Arendt, Eichmann in Jerusalem, 135–136.
9 Hick, *Christianity at the Centre*, 84, *Philosophy of Religion*, 41–42, *Evil and the God of Love*, 290.
10 Romans, 3:24–26; *Book of Common Prayer*, 11–12.
11 Galatians 1:4; *Book of Common Prayer*, 240–241.
12 Mark 14:33–42, 15:22–35.
13 Chadwick, 37; The Chalcedonian Definition; *Book of Common Prayer*, 240–241.
14 Mark 16:1–19.
15 Romans 5:1–21.

16 I Timothy 2:5–6; Colossians 1:14.
17 Whale, *Christian Doctrine*, 92–93; *A Handbook of Christian Theology*, 24–25; Robinson, *The Difference in Being a Christian Today,* 38–39; Jessop, *An Introduction to Christian Doctrine*, 62–63.
18 Lewis, *The Problem of Pain*, 103–104; Jeremy Bentham, *Principles of Morals and Legislation*, 29–33.
19 Bowker, *Problems of Suffering*, 92–93, 96; Philippians 2:6, 7, 8; Stein, *The Science of the Cross*, 30–31; Adams, *Philosophy of Religion: The Big Questions*, 256.
20 Mark 4:35–41, 6:30–44, 1:21–2:12.
21 Hume, *Enquiry*, 169–186; Flew and MacIntyre, *New Essays in Philosophical Theology*, 245–246; Barclay, *A Handbook of the Miracles of Jesus,* 24–32.
22 Hume, *Enquiry*, 136; Spinoza, *Theological-Political Treatise*, 57–69; Kant, *Religion,* 166, 98–101.
23 Butler, *Analogy,* 196–198; Swinburne, *The Existence of God*, 225–226, 232.
24 Lewis, *Miracles,* 87–98; Luke 1:26–31.
25 Mark 9:14–30; Matthew 6: 5–15.
26 *Book of Common Prayer*, 14–15, 313; Wiles, *God's Action in the World*, 107–108; *Catechism of the Catholic Church*, 71.
27 I John 4:9; Heiler, *Prayer*, 356–358; Buber, *I and Thou*, 100; Matthew 6:8; Luke 11:1; Stump, *Philosophy of Religion: The Big Questions*, 364.
28 Hick, *Philosophy of Religion*, 86.
29 Newman, *Grammar of Assent*, 225–250.

# FURTHER READING

This book introduces the basics of philosophical theology as it stands as an academic discipline or field of study within a broad Judaeo-Christian and Anglo-American analytic tradition.

The recommended further reading below is intended for the reader of this book, who, having grasped the basics as introduced here, wishes to continue their exploration of these topics into wider philosophical and theological traditions and fields.


Elizabeth Burns, *Continental Philosophy of Religion*. Cambridge: Cambridge University Press, 2019.

Colby Dickinson, 'Continental Philosophy and Theology', *Brill Research Perspectives in Theology*, *2*(1), 1–105, 2018.

Daniel H. Frank, 'Jewish Philosophical Theology', in eds. Thomas P. Flint, and Michael C. Rea, *The Oxford Handbook of Philosophical Theology* (Chapter 24). Oxford: Oxford University Press, 2011.

George F. Hourani, *Reason and Tradition in Islamic Ethics* (Chapter 1). Cambridge: Cambridge University Press, 1985.

Hisakazu Inagaki, and J. Nelson Jennings (eds.), *Philosophical Theology and East-West Dialogue*. Amsterdam: Brill, 2021.

Oliver Leaman, 'Islamic Philosophical Theology', in eds. Thomas P. Flint, and Michael C. Rea, *The Oxford Handbook of Philosophical Theology* (Chapter 25). Oxford: Oxford University Press, 2011.

Paul Mendes-Flohr, 'Jewish Philosophy and Theology', in ed. Martin Goodman, *The Oxford Handbook of Jewish Studies* (Chapter 30). Oxford: Oxford University Press, 2004.

R.W. Perrett (ed.), *Indian Philosophy of Religion*. Dordrecht: Kluwer, 1989.

Rafal K. Stepien, *Buddhism Between Religion and Philosophy: Nāgārjuna and the Ethics of Emptiness*. Oxford: Oxford University Press, 2024.

Rajeev Verma, *Faith & Philosophy of Hinduism*. Delhi: Kalpaz, 2009.

# BIBLIOGRAPHY


Adams, Marilyn McCord, 'Horrendous Evils and the Goodness of God', in Eleonore Stump and Michael J. Murray (eds.), *Philosophy of Religion: The Big Questions*. Oxford: Blackwell, 2004.

Anscombe, G.E.M., 'Modern Moral Philosophy', in W.D. Hudson (ed.), *The Is/Ought Question*. London: Macmillan, 1969.

Anselm, *Monologion and Proslogion with the Replies of Gaunilo and Anselm*, trans. T. Williams. Indianapolis: Hackett Publishing Company, 1995.

Aquinas, Thomas, *Basic Writings of Saint Thomas Aquinas*, vol. I, ed. A.C. Pegis. Indianapolis/Cambridge: Hackett Publishing Company, 1997.

Arendt, Hannah, *Eichmann in Jerusalem: A Report on the Banality of Evil*. London: Penguin, 2006.

Aristotle, *Metaphysics*, in Jonathan Barnes (ed.), *The Complete Works of Aristotle*, revised Oxford translation, vol. 2. Princeton: Princeton University Press, 1984.

Aristotle, *On the Soul*, in Jonathan Barnes (ed.), *The Complete Works of Aristotle*, revised Oxford translation, vol. 1. Princeton: Princeton University Press, 1984.

Augustine, *City of God*, trans. Henry Bettinger. Harmondsworth: Penguin, 1972.

Ayer, A.J., *Language, Truth and Logic*. Harmondsworth: Penguin, 1990.

Baillie, John, *Our Knowledge of God*. London: Geoffrey Cumberledge, Oxford University Press, 1952.

Baker, Lynne Rudder, 'Material Persons and the Doctrine of Resurrection', *Faith and Philosophy* 18(2), 2001.

Baker, Lynne Rudder, 'Resurrecting Material Persons', in Yujin Nagasawa and Benjamin Matheson (eds.), *The Palgrave Handbook of the Afterlife*. London: Palgrave Macmillan, 2017.

Barclay, William, *And He Had Compassion on Them: A Handbook of the Miracles of Jesus*. Edinburgh: The Church of Scotland Youth Committee, 1959.

Bentham, Jeremy, *An Introduction to the Principles of Morals and Legislation*. Mineola, NY: Dover, 2007.

Bonhoeffer, Dietrich, *Creation and Fall*, trans. J.C. Fletcher. London: SCM Press, 1959.
Bonhoeffer, Dietrich, *Christology*, trans. J. Bowden. London: Collins, 1966.
Bonhoeffer, Dietrich, *The Cost of Discipleship*, revised ed. London: SCM Press, 1969.
Bowker, John, *Problems of Suffering in Religions of the World*. Cambridge: Cambridge University Press, 1975.
Braithwaite, R.B., *An Empiricist's View of the Nature of Religious Belief.* Cambridge: Cambridge University Press, 1955.
Buber, Martin, *I and Thou*, trans. Ronald Gregor Smith, 2nd ed. London and New York: Continuum, 1958.
Butler, Joseph, *Butler's Analogy of Religion, Natural and Revealed*, ed. W.E. Gladstone. Oxford: Oxford University Press, 1907.
Butler, Joseph, *Five Sermons*, with 'A Dissertation Upon the Nature of Virtue', ed. S.L. Darwall. Indianapolis: Hackett Publishing Company, 1983.
Caird, G.B., *The Gospel of Saint Luke*. Harmondsworth: Penguin, 1963.
Calvin, John, *Institutes of the Christian Religion*, trans. H. Beveridge. Peabody, MA: Hendrickson, 2008.
Chadwick, Henry, *The Early Church*, Harmondsworth: Penguin, 1967
Clarke, Samuel and Leibniz, Gottfried Wilhelm, *The Leibniz–Clarke Correspondence*, ed. H.G. Alexander, Manchester: Manchester University Press, 1956.
Clarke, Samuel, *Third Defence of an Argument Made Use of in a Letter to Mr Dodwell.* London, 1708. Facsimile reprint, Gale ECCO Print Editions.
Clarke, Samuel, *A Letter to Mr Dodwell*. London, 1731. Facsimile reprint, Gale ECCO Print Editions.
Clifford, W.K., 'The Ethics of Belief', in Leslie Stephen and Frederick Pollock (eds.), *Lectures and Essays by the Late William Kingdon Clifford*, vol. 2. London: Macmillan, 1901.
Copleston, F.C., *Aquinas*. Harmondsworth: Penguin, 1991.
Copleston, F.C., and Russell, Bertrand, 'A Debate on the Existence of God', in John Hick (ed.), *The Existence of God*. London and New York: Macmillan, 1964.
Descartes, René, *Discourse on Method and Meditations on First Philosophy*, ed. D.A. Cress, 4th ed. Indianapolis/Cambridge: Hackett Publishing Company, 1998.
Fénelon, François, *The Maxims of the Saints Explained, Concerning the Interior Life*. London, 1698.
Fletcher, Joseph, *Situation Ethics*. London: SCM Press, 1966.
Flew, Antony, Hare, R.M., and Mitchell, Basil, 'Theology and Falsification', in Antony Flew and Alasdair MacIntyre (eds.), *New Essays in Philosophical Theology*. London: SCM Press, 1955.
Haroutunian, Joseph, 'Atonement', in M. Halverson and A. Cohen (eds.), *A Handbook of Christian Theology*. London: Fontana Books, 1960.
Hasker, William, *The Emergent Self.* Ithaca, NY: Cornell University Press, 1999.

Heiler, Friedrich, *Prayer*, trans. and ed. Samuel McComb. London and New York: Galaxy, 1958.

Hick, John, *Christianity at the Centre*. London: SCM Press, 1968.

Hick, John, *Philosophy of Religion*, 2nd ed. Englewood Cliffs, NJ: Prentice-Hall, 1973.

Hick, John, *Faith and Knowledge*, 2nd ed. London: Fontana, 1975.

Hick, John, *Evil and the God of Love*. London: Fount Paperbacks, 1979.

Hobbes, Thomas, *Leviathan*, ed. J.C.A. Gaskin. Oxford: Oxford University Press, 1998.

Hume, David, *Dialogues Concerning Natural Religion*, ed. Richard H. Popkin, 2nd ed. Indianapolis/Cambridge: Hackett Publishing Company, 1998.

Hume, David, *An Enquiry Concerning Human Understanding*, ed. T.L. Beauchamp. Oxford and New York: Oxford University Press, 1999.

Huxley, T.H., *Essays Upon Some Controverted Questions*. New York: D. Appleton and Company, 1892.

Huxley, T.H., 'Agnosticism: A Symposium', in eds. Naomi Hetherington, and Clare Stainthorp, N*ineteenth-Century Religion, Literature and Society: Disbelief and New Beliefs* (Chapter 41). Abingdon: Routledge, 2020

James, William, *The Varieties of Religious Experience*. New York and London: Longmans, Green, and Co., 1920.

James, William, *The Will to Believe and Other Essays in Popular Philosophy*. New York and London: Longmans, Green & Co., 1897. Reprint, CreateSpace Independent Publishing Platform, 2014.

Jeremias, Joachim, *The Sermon on the Mount*. Philadelphia: Fortress Press, 1973.

Jessop, T.E., *An Introduction to Christian Doctrine*. London: Thomas Nelson and Sons, 1960.

Jessop, T.E., *The Christian Morality*. London: The Epworth Press, 1960.

Kant, Immanuel, *Critique of Pure Reason*. London: Everyman, 1993.

Kant, Immanuel, *Groundwork of the Metaphysics of Morals*. Cambridge: Cambridge University Press, 1997.

Kant, Immanuel, *Religion within the Boundaries of Mere Reason*. Cambridge: Cambridge University Press, 1998.

Kant, Immanuel, *Critique of Practical Reason*. Indianapolis/Cambridge: Hackett Publishing Company, 2002.

Kierkegaard, Søren, *The Sickness unto Death*, trans. Walter Lowrie. Princeton, NJ: Princeton University Press, 1941.

Kierkegaard, Søren, *Philosophical Fragments*, trans. David F. Swenson. Princeton: Princeton University Press, 1957.

Kierkegaard, Søren, *Fear and Trembling*. Cambridge: Cambridge University Press, 2006.

Leibniz, Gottfried Wilhelm, 'The Monadology', in *The Rationalists*, trans. R.H.M. Elwes. New York: Dolphin Books, 1960.

Leibniz, Gottfried Wilhelm, *Theodicy*. Newton Stewart: Anodos Books, 2019.

Lewis, C.S., *The Problem of Pain*. London: The Centenary Press, 1941.

Lewis, C.S., *Miracles: A Preliminary Study*. London: William Collins, 2016.

Locke, John, *An Essay Concerning Human Understanding*. Oxford: Oxford University Press, 2008.

MacIntyre, Alasdair, 'Visions', in Antony Flew and Alasdair MacIntyre (eds.), *New Essays in Philosophical Theology*. London: SCM Press, 1955.

Mackie, J.L., 'Evil and Omnipotence', in Nelson Pike (ed.), *God and Evil*. Englewood Cliffs, NJ: Prentice-Hall, 1964.

Malcolm, Norman, 'Anselm's Ontological Arguments', in John Hick (ed.), *The Existence of God*. London and New York: Macmillan, 1964.

Masham, Damaris, *Occasional Thoughts in Reference to A Vertuous or Christian Life*. London: 1705. Reprint, Zinc Read, 2025.

McFague, Sallie, *Metaphorical Theology*. Philadelphia: Fortress Press, 1982.

Mercer, Christia, 'Descartes' Debt to Teresa of Ávila', *Philosophical Studies* 174(10), 2017.

Mill, John Stuart, 'Theism' and 'Nature', in *Three Essays on Religion*. New York: Prometheus Books, 1998.

Mill, John Stuart, *Utilitarianism*. Indianapolis/Cambridge: Hackett Publishing Company, 2001.

Moore, G.E., *Principia Ethica*. Cambridge: Cambridge University Press, 2000.

Newman, John Henry, *An Essay in Aid of a Grammar of Assent*, ed. N. Lash. Notre Dame, IN, and London: University of Notre Dame Press, 1979.

Niebuhr, Reinhold, *An Interpretation of Christian Ethics*. London: SCM Press, 1936.

Otto, Rudolf, *The Idea of the Holy*. Oxford: Oxford University Press, 1958.

Paley, William, *Natural Theology*. Oxford and New York: Oxford University Press, 2008.

Pascal, Blaise, *Pensées*. Harmondsworth: Penguin, 1966.

Plantinga, Alvin, 'Reason and Belief in God', in eds. A. Plantinga, Alvin, N.P. Wolterstorff, and P. Nicholas *Faith and Rationality: Reason and Belief in God*. Notre Dame: University of Notre Dame Press, 1983.

Plato, *Symposium*, in *Lysis, Symposium, Gorgias*, trans. W.R.M. Lamb. Cambridge, MA: Harvard University Press, 1925.

Plato, *The Republic*, in, eds. R.M. Hare and D.A. Russell, *The Dialogues of Plato*, trans. Benjamin Jowett, 4 Vols. London: Sphere Books, 1970.

Plato, *Defence of Socrates, Euthyphro, Crito*, trans. and ed. D. Gallop. Oxford and New York: Oxford University Press, 1997.

Pseudo-Dionysius, *The Divine Names and Mystical Theology*, trans. C.E. Rolt. London: SPCK, 1920.

Robinson, John A.T., *The Difference in Being a Christian Today*. London: Fontana, 1974.

Robinson, Richard, *An Atheist's Values*. Oxford: Oxford University Press, 1964.

Schleiermacher, Friedrich, *The Christian Faith*. Edinburgh: T. & T. Clark, 1928.

Smart, Ninian, 'Omnipotence, Evil and Supermen', in Nelson Pike (ed.), *God and Evil*. Englewood Cliffs, NJ: Prentice-Hall, 1964.

Soskice, Janet Martin, *Metaphor and Religious Language*. Oxford: Clarendon Press, 1985.

Spinoza, Benedict de, 'The Ethics', in *The Rationalists*, trans. Benjamin Jowett. New York: Dolphin Books, 1960.

Spinoza, Benedict de, *Theological-Political Treatise*, trans. R.H.M. Elwes. London: George Bell and Sons, 1883. Reprint, Anodos Books, 2019.

Stein, Edith (St Teresa Benedicta of the Cross), *The Science of the Cross*. Washington, DC: ICS Publications, 2018.

Stump, Eleonore, 'Petitionary Prayer', in Eleonore Stump and Michael J. Murray (eds.), *Philosophy of Religion: The Big Questions*. Oxford: Blackwell, 2004.

Swinburne, Richard, *The Existence of God*, revised ed. Oxford: Oxford University Press, 1991.

Temple, William, *Readings in St John's Gospel*. London: Macmillan, 1939.

Teresa of Ávila, *The Life of Teresa of Jesus*, trans. David Lewis. London: Thomas Baker, 1904.

Tolstoy, Leo, *My Religion: What I Believe*. Guildford: White Crow Books, 2009.

Voltaire, *Candide*, trans. John Butt. Harmondsworth: Penguin, 1978.

Warnock, G.J., *The Object of Morality*. London: Methuen, 1971.

Whale, J.S., *Christian Doctrine*. London: Fontana, 1960.

Wiles, Maurice, *God's Action in the World*. London: SCM Press, 1986.

Wisdom, John, 'Gods', in John Hick (ed.), *Philosophy of Religion*. Englewood Cliffs, NJ: Prentice-Hall, 1973.

Wittgenstein, Ludwig, *Tractatus Logico-Philosophicus*. London: Routledge & Kegan Paul, 1922.

Wittgenstein, Ludwig, *Philosophical Investigations*. Oxford: Blackwell, 1958.

Wittgenstein, Ludwig, *Lectures and Conversations*. Oakland: University of California Press, 1966.

Wittgenstein, Ludwig, *Zettel*. Oxford: Blackwell, 1967.

Wittgenstein, Ludwig, *On Certainty*. New York: Harper & Row, 1969.

Wittgenstein, Ludwig, *Culture and Value*. Chicago: University of Chicago Press, 1980.

Zagzebski, Linda, *Virtues of the Mind*. Cambridge: Cambridge University Press, 1996.

Zagzebski, Linda, *Epistemic Authority*. Oxford: Oxford University Press, 2012.

*The Bible: Revised Standard Version*. London and New York: Collins, 1973.

*The Book of Common Prayer*. Cambridge: Cambridge University Press, 1961.

*The Chalcedonian Creed*. https://anglicansonline.org

# INDEX

For Product Safety Concerns and Information please contact our EU representative GPSR@taylorandfrancis.com
Taylor & Francis Verlag GmbH, Kaufingerstraße 24, 80331 München, Germany

www.ingramcontent.com/pod-product-compliance
Lightning Source LLC
LaVergne TN
LVHW021259120926
847938LV00037B/839

*9781032939759*